HOW SAINTS DIE

ANTONIO MARIA SICARI

HOW SAINTS DIE
100 Stories of Hope

TRANSLATED BY
MATTHEW SHERRY

IGNATIUS PRESS   SAN FRANCISCO

Original Italian edition: *Come muoiono i santi*
International copyright © 2016 Edizioni Ares, Milano, Italy
All rights reserved
This English edition has been produced by arrangement with
Silvia Vassena © Milano Consulting & Scouting

Cover photograph of Cala Lily
© iStock/tsvibrav

Cover design by Enrique J. Aguilar

© 2021 by Ignatius Press, San Francisco
All rights reserved
ISBN 978-1-62164-449-1 (PB)
ISBN 978-1-64229-167-4 (eBook)
Library of Congress Control Number 2021933131
Printed in the United States of America ∞

Contents

"Won't it be a bit gloomy to read, this book?" a friend said to me, glancing at the title of the manuscript (which I had just finished) on the table.

I thought back on a play by Gustave Thibon (significantly entitled *You Will Be Like Gods!*)[1] that portrays the jubilation of a society where man has become immortal: science and technological progress have finally brought victory over nature! Just one young woman finds herself in the grip of an overwhelming sadness. "Aren't you happy?" her friends ask her in amazement. "Don't you understand that we have toppled the wall of death?" But she remains pensive: "And if, instead of toppling a wall, we have closed a door? I don't want this immortality, because I need eternity."

Sooner or later—the author concluded—we will have to decide whether we want to be men of the future or men of eternity.

The difference is in the tremulous desire of Saint Teresa of Ávila, who was already saying as a little girl, "I want to see God!"

In this book, therefore, I have recounted the death of many saints, but all of them have confirmed for me the truth of this ancient Christian intuition: in the death of a saint, it is death that dies!

—Father Antonio Maria Sicari, O.C.D.

[1] *Vous serez comme des dieux* (Paris: Fayard, 1954).

INTRODUCTION

Death, Love, Holiness

There are two fundamental experiences in our human existence: love and suffering. With the word *love*, we can summarize all the good we receive and give over the course of our lives. With the word *suffering*, we intend to evoke here all the evil undergone in body and soul, which seems to come to a head when the onslaught of maladies and pains tells us that death is near: the dissolution of our very *self*. And between love and suffering an inevitable appointment is always lying in wait.

Suffering poses questions, and love makes a promise

Suffering forces man to ask himself that radical question, "Who am I?", which accompanies us our whole life long (together with other questions on why we exist and on the purpose of living) but becomes urgent and intense when we no longer have anyone to hold on to.

Of course, our experiences over the years may have left us with many reflections, many convictions, and many "certainties of faith", but all of these (in order to be given and for us to perceive them) have to come to us through persons who bear the response that comes first and last: "You are the being that I love!"

Normally this response is entrusted at first to those who have given us life and become responsible for protecting it (parents, relatives) and then to those who have given us their loving companionship (spouse, children, friends).

Evidently mother and spouse are the only two persons who have been able to respond to us even with their flesh.

Over the course of the years, the substantial dialogue to which we have referred (Who am I?—You are the being that I love!), even if it is expressed tacitly, is enough to satisfy and reassure us even when we waver (as long as we have the grace and happiness of being able to savor it!).

The response, when it is true, always comes to us as a grace of consolation: one who feels loved intuits right away that this contains many other promises but waits for time to manifest and realize them.

But when the time of extreme suffering arrives and the self senses the decisive threat of death, then the perennial question (Who am I?) grows infinitely larger and demands a response that is just as decisive.

One feels how urgent it is that the promise contained in every expression of love finally be made explicit.

Here it is: "He who loves says, You will never die!" Gabriel Marcel puts these words in the mouth of Arnaud Chartain, the main character of his play *La soif*.[1] In another of his works on the *Mystery of Being*, he explained it like this: "What could the precise meaning of that statement be? It certainly cannot be reduced to a wish or even a desire, but it has instead the character of a prophetic pledge. . . . Its exact formulation could be this: no matter what changes I may see, you and I will stay together; [what has happened] cannot impair the promise of eternity included in our love."[2]

---

[1] *La soif (Pièce en trois actes)* (Paris: Desclée de Brouwer, 1935).

[2] *Le mystère de l'être*, vol. 2, *Foi et réalité* (Paris: Aubier, 1981), pp. 154–55. G. Marcel had already foreshadowed this in *Homo viator* (Paris: Aubier, 1944), p. 189.

We could add that, if we were to encapsulate all the expressions of true love that men exchange with one another, this would be nothing other than "the enchanting promise that Love makes to humanity on God's behalf".[3] But here is where the most mysterious paradox emerges: just when the fulfillment of this promise cannot be put off any longer, it is just then we discover that in human terms the promise *cannot* be kept. It is not that the promise was false or insincere. On the contrary, it was and is necessary, because it belongs intrinsically to the nature of love. It is simply that earthly lovers are unable to keep it: they do not have the power, in the face of death, no matter how great and sincere their love may be.

Jesus Christ: The one who keeps the promise

But this is just what God has left us with as our strongest inducement to appeal to Him!

When we creatures cannot fulfill the promise contained within our own love (since we ourselves are mortal), the promise is not shown to be false; rather, it turns into an appeal.

When it comes to promises of love, who can truly respond if not He who is Love: Love Crucified and Risen?

If Jesus is Love made flesh, it is also up to Him to fulfill the promises of love! This is the most evident proof of the need we have for His presence and His grace.

So when deep within our hearts we feel an aching over the infinite promises our frailty makes us unable to guarantee even though they are necessary, this means the decisive

[3] E. Caffarel, *Pensieri sull'amore e la grazia* (Milan: Istituto La casa, 1963), p. 48.

moment has come to accept in an absolutely unique and personal way that invitation which Pope John Paul II issued right away—as soon as he was elected—to the whole world: "Be not afraid! Christ knows what is in the heart of man. He alone knows."

And he would continue to issue it, insistently, above all to young people: "Christ is therefore the one competent interlocutor to whom you can put the essential questions about the value and meaning of life, not only a healthy, happy life, but also a life weighed down by suffering. . . . Yes, even for tragic problems which can be expressed more by groans than by words, Christ is the competent interlocutor. Ask him, listen to him!"[4]

When the moment of death comes, it will be important to have a good and longstanding familiarity with the Gospel descriptions of the Passion of Jesus.

The saints contemplated these often, also discovering in them—full of astonishment—the account of their own sufferings (incorporated in advance into those of Christ) and even the desire for their own death.[5]

Already Saint Paul could give testimony to the first Christians: "I bear on my body the marks of Jesus" (Gal 6:17), and he was convinced that the pains of his existence (above all, those connected to his countless missionary efforts and the persecutions he underwent)[6] were for him a very special form of grace: "But far be it from me to glory except in the cross of our Lord Jesus Christ, by which the world has been crucified to me, and I to the world" (Gal 6:14).

---

[4] Pope St. John Paul II, address at Youth Vigil, 3.1, at World Youth Day in Compostela, Saturday, August 19, 1989.

[5] "Muero porque no muero" (I die because I do not die!) is used as a refrain in some of the poems of St. Teresa of Ávila and St. John of the Cross.

[6] Cf. 2 Cor 11:23-27.

He said he had no other goal in this world but "that I may know him and the power of his resurrection, and may share his sufferings, becoming like him in his death, that if possible I may attain the resurrection from the dead" (Phil 3:10–11) and felt the responsibility of filling up in his flesh what was lacking in the Passion of Christ (cf. Col 1:24).

Pope Saint Leo the Great explained: "True reverence for the Lord's passion means fixing the eyes of our heart on Jesus crucified and recognizing in him our own humanity."[7]

In all the Passion accounts (that of Christ and those of His saints, above all of His martyrs), we do not find explanations for our questions about suffering and death, but we do find the certainty that the Son of God came to keep us company even in suffering.

Jesus will never leave us to suffer alone and will unite Himself completely with us, precisely in the final moment of death: "None of us lives to himself, and none of us dies to himself. If we live, we live to the Lord, and if we die, we die to the Lord; so then, whether we live or whether we die, we are the Lord's" (Rom 14:7–8).

How infinitely consoling it is to discover in the Gospel that our death will take place within an agreement of love already stipulated between the Father and the Son: "All that the Father gives me will come to me; . . . this is the will of him who sent me, that I should lose nothing of all that he has given me, but raise it up at the last day. For this is the will of my Father, that every one who sees the Son and believes in him should have eternal life; and I will raise him up at the last day" (Jn 6:37–40)!

[7] Leo the Great, Sermo 15 on the Passion of the Lord, 3–4, *Patrologia Latina* 54, 366–67, in *The Liturgy of the Hours*, Thursday, Fourth Week of Lent (New York: Catholic Book Publishing, 1976), 2:313.

Every believer should ask for the grace to be buried with this page of the Gospel clutched in his hands.

The experience of the saints

The saints did not fear death.

Some of them died prematurely, at a young age, almost consumed by an impatient love for God and also, I would dare to say, *on the part of God*. Others almost provoked it—but without arrogance—because of the martyrial urgency of bearing witness to Christ: His Life and His Truth.

Some desired it in a mystical impetus of the heart that drove them to pray that the Bridegroom Christ might hasten His coming. Some awaited and experienced it with extreme suffering, but because they were called by love to relive the dramatic hours of Good Friday.

Some almost "sought" it in the vehemence of consuming themselves entirely in "works and works" of charity and mission. Others tasted it in old age, "full of days", happily weary from their lifelong labors in the vineyard of the Lord.

We can say this procession of Christian saints who went to their deaths in peace was opened—when Jesus was still just a few days old—by the elderly Saint Simeon, who prayed to be allowed to depart in peace after his arms had been able to clasp the holy Child and his eyes had finally "seen salvation".

This is what Christian hope is: going to meet death with the joyful assurance of embracing Life, after having the chance on earth to contemplate the Seed of Salvation.

CHAPTER I

Dying as Martyrs

We can respond adequately to Jesus, the Son of God who gave His very life for us, only by giving our whole existence.

In times of peace and of joyful growth, this proceeds according to the rhythm of the life of faith, as the believer gradually learns the demands of Christian discipleship.

In times of persecution (usually those in which the ecclesial community is being founded or in which the secular world grows hardened and lashes out against it), the gift of life can be asked of all believers, at any moment, and the necessary maturation is a gift from God that accompanies and sustains the call to martyrdom itself.

This does not change the fact that there are historical circumstances (as in the early centuries) in which the *praeparatio martyrii* (preparation for martyrdom) is the most adequate form of pedagogy. It is, then, a matter of teaching the Christian faithful not only to belong to the Lord Jesus in life, but to belong to Him in death: a death always imminent as the ultimate and most glorious affirmation of their *spiritual identity*.

The ancient *Acts of the Martyrs* tell us how at times some of them went so far as to refuse to give their names to the persecutors, seeing as more than sufficient the name of *Christian* for which they had been imprisoned.

The cry of Saint Paul, "It is no longer I who live, but Christ who lives in me", must come true for all Christians, and this usually happens in the mysterious depths of the baptized self, into which the believer plunges all the more deeply the more he "believes".

In the martyrs, however, this cry (with which the self strives to evoke the very Person of Christ) rises to the surface of their being, and the power of His Presence must become *visible*.

Placed before the "serious case" of the most radical testimony, the martyrs tell the world that a life without Christ is dead, while death with Christ is for them eternal life.

"Giving one's life" or "losing it intentionally" is not yet *martyrdom*, even if this name has sometimes been applied to the experience of generous men who have sacrificed themselves for their country or for a just cause or even to guarantee a more certain and large-scale destruction of the enemy.

A Christian martyr is such on only two conditions. In the first place, his "strength" must not be a human display of grit. Even if this is possible in some cases (by resorting to all the techniques of courage and resistance), the Christian martyr, instead, openly counts upon his weakness in order to hand it over to an Other and let Him take care of it. The Christian who is led to martyrdom or, worse, to the unbearable torture that precedes it is asked only to make it *with faith* to the threshold of the unbearable, *believing* that Christ (*his true "self"*), will suffer it in his place.

Thus, the *Authentic Acts of the Martyrdom of Saints Felicity and Perpetua* (traditionally attributed to Tertullian) readily present the episode of the young martyr Felicity, forced to give birth in prison and mocked during this by her jailers ("If you're crying so much now, what will you do when we throw you to the beasts?"). She responds with humble assurance, "Now it is I who suffer, but there it will be an Other who suffers for me!"

The martyr must also die without the slightest trace of

hatred or rancor for his persecutors, but almost dragging them along—in his forgiveness, in his love, and in his hope —by offering himself on behalf of an ineffable communion between saints and sinners, which reestablishes the bonds precisely where evil would like to shatter them forever.

The martyrs, in essence, know they are *already risen with Christ*, precisely as they are being called by grace to *complete His Passion in their own members*.

~

The first centuries of Christian history are rich with examples of martyrs that tradition has commemorated with affection, and many of those ancient names have become dear to us.

Already the historian Tacitus wrote that under Nero an "enormous multitude" of Christians were killed. And the Christian authors speak of "a great multitude of the elect" or of "a countless throng of witnesses".

The catacombs (of Saint Callixtus, of Saint Domitilla, of Priscilla, of Saint Sebastian, of Saint Agnes) have preserved their sacred memory.

In this text, however, we prefer to evoke once again some of the martyrs from the second millennium, who lived in sociopolitical contexts closer to our own.

Saint Thomas Becket
(1118–1170)

Saint Thomas Becket marked the beginning of the second millennium, choosing to "love the honor of God" more than the devotion and friendship that he felt for his king,

Henry II, keeping him from domineering over the English Church.

In court, in an outburst of rage, the king had exclaimed, "What miserable drones and traitors have I nurtured and promoted in my household, who let their lord be treated with such shameful contempt by a low-born cleric!" This was enough to get four indignant knights to swear an oath to avenge their sovereign. They arrived in Canterbury with an armed escort on the afternoon of December 29, 1170, when the archbishop was preparing to celebrate vespers. Although he could have barricaded himself inside the cathedral, he ordered that the doors be kept open: "It is not proper that a house of prayer, a church of Christ, should be turned into a fortress!" he said. Or he could have hidden in the crypt, but he decided to stay by the altar, dressed in solemn episcopal vestments and holding a cross in his hand. The conspirators brandished swords and axes.

"Where is Thomas Becket, traitor of the king and kingdom?" they shouted.

"Here I am, not a traitor of the king but a priest", replied the archbishop, gazing steadily at the statue of the holy Virgin that stood on the wall in front of him.

And as the group fell upon him, Thomas covered his eyes with his hands and murmured, "Into your hands, Lord, I commend my spirit."

Then he firmly added, "For the name of Jesus and the protection of the Church, I am ready to embrace death."

They hit him on the head with an ax, and he fell in a pool of blood. And before going to sack the episcopal residence, the conspirators ordered that the body be thrown into a swamp. The news of the murder shook Europe. It was said even the pope was troubled and withdrawn, so much so that for eight days no one dared speak to him. And that Henry II himself kept to his chambers for three days, refusing food.

The tragic death in defense of the Church's freedom that Thomas underwent in the cathedral, dressed in pontifical vestments and in the course of a sacred liturgy, made such an impression on his contemporaries that he was even given the grandiose title of *Archbishop Primate not only of a city, but of the whole world.*

He was canonized in 1173, just two years after his death, and was already depicted among the holy martyrs in the mosaics in the semi-dome of the apse in the cathedral of Monreale, built in 1174.

Saint Thomas More
(1478–1535)

Born in London, Thomas More was one of the greatest humanists of his time. He is the author of a famous work of political philosophy entitled *Utopia.* Married and the father of four children, he worked as a lawyer and demonstrated intense charity, even founding a *House of Providence* for infirm elderly people and children.

In 1529, he was appointed by King Henry VIII to be Lord Chancellor of England (as Thomas Becket had been before him). Unfortunately, the king was at odds with the pope; he was demanding the annulment of his marriage with Catherine of Aragon (who had not given him a son) so he could marry Anne Boleyn. When the pontiff refused, the king had himself proclaimed "sole protector and supreme head of the Church of England". Unable to accept this decision in good conscience, More resigned from his office as chancellor.

Imprisoned in the Tower of London, he stayed there for fifteen months, meditating on the Passion of Christ and "seeking to follow humbly in His footsteps". To those who tried to change his mind, pointing out that many bishops had accepted the Act of Supremacy, Thomas replied, "If I should speak of those that are already dead, of whom many be now holy saints in heaven, I am very sure it is the far greater part of them that, all the while they lived, thought in this case that way that I think now; and therefore I am not bounden, my lord, to conform my conscience to the Council of one realm against the general council of Christendom."

He was beheaded on Tower Hill on July 6, 1535, the vigil of the feast of Saint Thomas Becket. The day before he had written to his daughter, "Tomorrow long I to go to God, it were a day very meet and convenient for me." And just as the first Thomas had decided his last words would be those of Stephen the Protomartyr, so also More addressed the judges who had just condemned him, evoking the same biblical episode: "More have I not to say, my lords, but that like as the blessed apostle Saint Paul, as we read in the Acts of the Apostles, was present and consented to the death of Saint Stephen, and kept their clothes that stoned him to death, and yet be they now both twain holy saints in heaven and shall continue there friends together forever, so I verily trust, and shall therefore heartily pray, that, though your lordships have now here on the earth been judges to my condemnation, we may yet hereafter in heaven merrily all meet together to our everlasting salvation."

In this way he died a Christian death. Throughout his life, he had exalted the dignity of man—as advanced by the Renaissance—while harmonizing faith, culture, charity, family affections, social and political engagement. In the end, by dying as a martyr, he showed that his highest dignity lay in the ability to give his life completely to Jesus Christ.

With Thomas More, in addition, the humanistic ideal of the *true man* not only affirmed itself in the face of persecution and death, but it reached a lofty peak: that of recognizing the full dignity of one's own persecutors, to the point of wishing them, with true hope, nothing less than sainthood, making a date with them in heaven.

We shall now jump ahead to the end of the eighteenth century, when it will no longer be kings who are making martyrs of Christians, but "citizens" claiming to act in the name of "liberty, equality, and fraternity".

Blessed Carmelite Martyrs of Compiègne
(1794)

At the end of 1793, the French revolutionaries unleashed the *great terror* in the name of their "enlightened reason" that demanded "not only the punishment, but the annihilation of the enemies of the homeland", in addition to "its complete dechristianization".

But in order to condemn sixteen Carmelite nuns to death, they could find no "reasonable light" other than to accuse them of *fanaticism*.

Thus sixteen women were guillotined in Paris, in what was called at the time "Toppled Throne Square", in the name of the Republic (and to think that two of them were almost eighty years old!).

But the nuns were able to turn the horrible scene into a liturgical action, and the crowd behaved as if they were at a sacred ceremony. Usually the convoys of the condemned had to make their way through a noisy, drunken gauntlet, but witnesses say the two carts into which the nuns had been loaded passed through "a crowd so silent there was no other like it during the Revolution".

It was around eight in the evening when they came to the old square where the guillotine was set up. The prioress got permission from the executioner to be the last to die, so that as mother she could assist and support all of her religious, especially the youngest. They wanted to die together, in spiritual terms as well, as if they were performing a unique and final act as a community. The prioress also asked the executioner for a slight delay, which he again granted, whereupon she intoned the *Veni Creator Spiritus*, and they sang it all the way through. Then they renewed their vows. After this the mother superior stood off to the side of the guillotine, holding in the hollow of her hand a little clay figurine of the holy Virgin that she had managed to keep hidden.

The first was the young novice, who knelt before the prioress, asked for her blessing and for permission to die, kissed the figurine of the Virgin, and climbed the steps of the guillotine "as happy as if she were going to a party", witnesses said. While she was mounting the steps, she intoned the psalm *Laudate Dominum omnes gentes*, which was taken up by the others, who followed her one after another with the same peace and the same joy, even if the more elderly nuns had to be helped up. Last came the prioress, after giving the figurine to someone who was standing nearby (it is still kept to this day at the monastery of Compiègne).

Emmanuel Renault writes: "The thud of the counterweight, the hollow sound of the cut, the muffled sound of the falling head. . . . Not a shout, no applause or rowdy yelling (as was usually the case). Even the drums were silent. Over this square, tainted with the smell of fetid blood, rotten with the summer heat, a solemn hush fell over those in attendance, and perhaps the prayer of the Carmelites had already touched their hearts."

It would later become known that more than one of the young women who were there that day promised to God, in their hearts, to take their places.

This touching episode was turned into a novella (*The Song at the Scaffold*, by Gertrud von Le Fort), which was in turn made into a play (*The Fearless Heart*, by Georges Bernanos), an opera (*Dialogues of the Carmelites*, by Francis Poulenc), and a film (*Le Dialogue des Carmélites*, written and directed by Raymond Bruckberger and Philippe Agostini).

Blessed Miguel Agustín Pro
(1891–1927)

Recent studies say that in the twentieth century—which saw the mutual opposition, the succession, or the coexistence of the most violent revolutionary ideologies—there were more than forty-five million Christian martyrs.

Leading the ranks was the young Jesuit priest Miguel Agustín Pro, victim of the first great persecution of the century, which broke out in Mexico at the instigation of Masonic groups that in 1917 enacted the first socialist constitution in world history, with the explicit intention of completely uprooting the Catholic faith from the country and from consciences.

It came to the point that all the priests were forced underground. Father Miguel Pro thus became "God's play-actor", employing his skills of mimicry and imagination for the sake of engaging with and sustaining the faithful any way he could.

He exercised his ministry in hiding and with unflagging

energy, resorting to ingenious disguises in order to evade police surveillance and preaching courses of spiritual exercises in secret. He founded *Eucharistic centers* where every day he distributed Communion for hundreds, even for up to 1,500 in a single day. He also knew how to cheer up the people with the guitar and by organizing celebrations. After just two years of priesthood, he was arrested under the false accusation of having participated in a political assassination attempt. The trial was carried out with absolute contempt for legal norms and human rights, and Father Miguel was sentenced to the firing squad.

He was executed in the presence of journalists and photographers, because the dictator in power at the time wanted to offer the world the spectacle of a frightened priest begging for mercy. Instead, it was a sacred celebration.

When, on the morning of November 23, 1927, the door of the underground prison was opened and the warden's voice called out his name, Father Pro understood his hour had come. He stopped for a moment to bless his fellow prisoners, and his guard, who was weeping, asked for his forgiveness.

"Not only do I forgive you, but I thank you", the priest replied, and embraced him.

When he reached the place of execution, he was allowed to express the traditional last wish, and he asked for a little time to pray. He did so on his knees, in front of the firing squad.

Then he got up and said, "God is my witness that I am innocent of the crime with which they have charged me. May the Lord have mercy on you all."

He extended his arms in the form of a cross, holding a crucifix in one hand and a rosary in the other, and added, "I forgive my enemies with all my heart."

And then, in a loud voice, "Viva Cristo Rey!"

It appears one of the soldiers on the firing squad murmured in distress, "This is how the just die!"

And the photos the dictator had meant to be used to humiliate the martyr were immediately passed around as relics.

A few days before he died, Father Pro had written this heartrending prayer for himself: "I believe, O Lord; but strengthen my faith. Heart of Jesus, I love Thee; but increase my love. Heart of Jesus, I trust in Thee, but give greater vigor to my confidence. Heart of Jesus, I give my heart to Thee; but so enclose it in Thee that it may never be separated from Thee. Heart of Jesus, I am all Thine; but take care of my promise so that I may be able to put it in practice even unto the complete sacrifice of my life."[1]

Blessed Vladimir Ghika
(1873–1954)

He belongs to the countless ranks of martyrs who bore witness to the faith before the rage of the atheistic socio-communist regimes. He was a Romanian prince who converted to Catholicism and was declared a martyr in 2013.

At the beginning of the tormented twentieth century, he —who would go on to become a priest—founded his country's first Catholic institute dedicated to works of charity, inspired by Saint Vincent de Paul. He expended all of his energy and all of his belongings for the poor and sick, but also developed a distinctive "liturgy of the neighbor", which became a constant feature of his thinking and of the formation he imparted to his followers.

---

[1] M. D. Forrest, *The Life of Father Pro* (St. Paul, Minn.: Radio Replies Press, 1945), p. 115.

"Liturgy of the neighbor" means that in visiting the poor, one must celebrate "the encounter of Jesus with Jesus". In fact, "on both sides there is only Christ: Christ the Savior comes to Christ the Suffering, and both are united in Christ risen, glorious, and full of blessing."

So Vladimir, when he was called to meet some sort of need, went on his way praying, "Lord, I am going to meet one of those you have called your 'other self'." This was his favorite maxim: "Nothing brings God so close as one's neighbor", and he put this into practice to the last hour of his life, even amid the horror of the communist prison into which he was thrown when he was more than eighty years old and where he spent his last months sustaining all the other prisoners with the affection, the attentiveness, and the storytelling of an elderly grandfather.

He was thus able to apply, literally, what he had jotted down in his *Thoughts*, commenting on the episode of the disciples of Emmaus: "When the day is dying, the disciples of Jesus can be recognized only by the way in which—like their Teacher—they are able to break bread, sacrificing for their brothers the living bread of their own bodies."

In prison, he broke this bread by using up for the sake of his fellow prisoners the remnants of his feeble voice. During the long, freezing nighttime hours, they would all be hanging on his every word, never tired of asking him for a story that would illuminate and warm the darkness of that terrible prison. Vladimir had an insider's knowledge of the glorious history of the ancient Romanian principalities; he had frequented the royal families of almost all the countries in the world; he had got to know four popes and had lived in the Vatican and in the Holy City; he had traveled over all the continents; he had frequented the salons of the intellectuals and the studios of the most famous artists.

The prisoners would gather around him like impatient children, "Monsignor, please, another story!"

And Vladimir would speak at length, recounting, describing, depicting anecdotes and personages from real life, mixing his narrative with reflections on suffering, on holiness, on one's neighbor, on God. The prison walls seemed to disappear, and the prisoners began to believe again in life, in history, in the beauty of the world, in the Divine Providence that penetrated even those cold and foul-smelling walls. "For him," one witness recounted, "the prison walls did not exist. He was free, because he was doing God's will."

This is how, in that prison warmed only by the charity of that elderly priest, the terrible winter between 1953 and 1954 passed. When springtime came, Ghika was spent. He was taken to the prison infirmary—where they left him half-naked—and he died there all alone on May 16, 1954. He had said prophetically, "Our death must be the supreme act of our life: but it may happen that God is the only one who knows about it."

Saint Maximilian Kolbe
(1894-1941)

He was a young Polish Conventual Franciscan, full of apostolic ardor and of initiative, who had founded in his country a community named *Niepokalanów*, the City of the Immaculate. At first, this consisted of a large Marian basilica, followed by a friary for hundreds of friars (there were 762 after ten years) and a publishing house equipped with all the necessary features. It even had a train station and a little airport.

He was arrested by the Nazis at the height of his apostolic

activity, which by that time reached all the way to Japan. He looked at the concentration camp as a new mission field. During choosing of ten victims, which the commandant of the camp had decided on after a prisoner escaped, Father Kolbe volunteered to take the place of one of the victims, who was desperately calling out about his wife and children.

They were condemned to die of starvation and were thrown naked into the death bunker, where nothing was given to them, not even a drop of water. But from that day forward, the camp possessed a sacred place. The long agony was punctuated by the prayers and sacred hymns Father Kolbe recited and sang out loud. And from the cells nearby, the other victims would respond.

The story of what was happening spread to other concentration camps.

Every morning, the starvation bunker was inspected. When the cells were opened, those poor prisoners were weeping and asking for bread. Those who approached the guards were struck and thrown violently to the cement floor. Father Kolbe did not ask for anything, did not complain, remained seated on the floor, leaning against the wall. Even the soldiers regarded him with respect.

Then those who had been condemned began to die; after two weeks, there were only four left alive, including Father Kolbe. On August 14, 1941, they were given an injection of carbolic acid in their left arms to speed up their deaths. It was the vigil of one of Maximilian's most beloved Marian feasts: the Assumption, for which he was always eager to sing the popular hymn that says, "I am going to see her, one day!"

One of the guards said afterward, "When I reopened the iron door, he was not alive anymore, but he looked as if he were. Still leaning against the wall. The face was unusually radiant. The eyes opened wide and concentrated on one point. The whole figure as if in an ecstasy. I will never forget it."

Father Maximilian had been the last to die, bearing witness that faith and charity had brought victory precisely where the destruction of man's very humanity had been planned. He was canonized as a "martyr of charity".

Blessed Franz Jägerstätter
(1907–1943)

He was a simple Austrian farmer, born on the border with Belgium, but he dared to oppose Hitler's regime, refusing to collaborate in any way. Called to arms, he refused to enlist because in conscience he could not participate in an unjust war. He had studied the Bible and the documents of the Church and had spoken with friends and with educated persons, so his conviction had become unshakeable. Even his parish priest had to admit, "He left me speechless, because he had the better arguments. We wanted to get him to give up, but he always got the better of us by citing the Scriptures."

He fought against Nazism, concerned that his little girls would have to live in a dechristianized world (which was exactly what Nazism was aiming for, from the earliest years of childhood). For this he was imprisoned and killed at the age of thirty-six.

To his wife, who supported him faithfully in his difficult decision of conscience, and to his daughters, he left this testament: "Although I am writing . . . in chains, this is still much better than if my will were in chains. . . . Not prison, not chains, and not even death are capable of separating people from the love of God, robbing them of their faith and free will."[2]

And in the last letter he was able to send to them, he wrote: "It was not possible for me to free both of you from the sorrows that you have suffered for me. . . . I thank our Savior that I could suffer for him and may die for him."[3] And he concluded with these words: "Heart of Jesus, heart of Mary, and my heart be one heart bound for time and eternity."[4]

During his last days, he found comfort in the Eucharist he received frequently from the prison chaplain, his daily Bible readings, and a photo of his daughters.

His fellow prisoners recounted afterward that Franz had become so charitable he often went without his last piece of bread, giving it instead to those who were most worn-out. One of these would later write to Jägerstätter's wife: "The children have every right to believe that their father died as a saint." And the chaplain would write: "Rest assured that few in Germany have died as your husband did. He died as a hero, as a believer, as a martyr, and as a saint."

To the very end, a form was left on the table for him, with which he could have taken an oath to serve in the German army. He could have saved his life with a signature. But to the prison chaplain, who visited him to comfort him and tried to draw his attention to that sheet, he replied, "I cannot . . . My soul is bound fast to the Lord."

---

[2] *Franz Jägerstätter: Letters and Writings from Prison*, ed. Erna Putz, trans. Robert A. Krieg (Maryknoll, N.Y.: Orbis Books, 2009), p. 243.

[3] Ibid., p. 129.

[4] Ibid., p. 130.

Blessed Titus Brandsma
(1881–1942)

He was a Dutch Carmelite priest—professor of philosophy and of the history of mysticism at the Catholic University of Nijmegen, of which he was also rector—who was deported and killed by the Nazis in the Dachau concentration camp.

Already in 1936, when the news was not yet so widespread or clear, he had contributed to a pamphlet entitled *Stemmen von Nederlanders over de Behandeling der Joden in Duitschland* (Dutch voices on the treatment of the Jews in Germany), writing: "What is now done against the Jews is an act of cowardice. The enemies and adversaries of the Jews are certainly so narrow minded that they think they have to act like this, act in this way. To think that they consequently reveal or strengthen the power of the people, is 'the illusion of weakness'."[5]

Right away there were angry reactions in Germany, where the national press called him "a spiteful professor".

But Brandsma, aware of his responsibility as an educator, did not give up. During the academic year of 1938–1939, he was already offering his students courses on the "menacing tendencies" of national socialism, in which he addressed all the key issues: the value and dignity of every single human person (healthy or sick); the equality and goodness of every race; the indestructible and primary value of natural law in comparison with any ideology; the presence and guidance

[5] As translated and quoted by the Titus Brandsma Institute, Nijmegen, website on the "Writings of Titus Brandsma": titusbrandsmateksten.nl/titus -brandsma-and-his-speech-on-the-occasion-of-handing-over-the-rectorship/# cite_ref-22.

of God in human history, against any political messianism
and any idolatry of power.

And he knew that among his hearers were partisan spies.

In 1941, a controversy erupted in Holland: Should Catholic newspapers publish notices from the National Socialist
Movement in the Netherlands, or not? In his capacity as
ecclesiastical assistant for Catholic publications, Titus sent
a memo rejecting all collaboration in the name of the Catholic press as a whole. It went unheeded.

A few months later, Brandsma was arrested and deported
to Dachau, where he was subjected to all sorts of abuse and
to actual torture.

When he had to be sent to the hospital section of the
camp, his fate was sealed. We now know what happened
from an exceptional witness: the very one who killed him
and then later converted, because the memory of Father Titus would not let her be.

She worked as a nurse, but out of fear she obeyed the
inhuman orders of the medical official. She was the one
who recounted that "when [Titus] arrived in the infirmary
he was already on the list of the dead." She was the one
who recounted the experiments that were carried out on
the patients, including Titus, and how, without her wanting it, the words with which he endured his mistreatment
were etched inside her, "Father, not my will, but yours be
done."

She was the one who recounted how all the patients hated
her and always insulted her with the most degrading names,
a hatred she heartily returned; and how she was stunned
because that elderly priest, instead, treated her with the tenderness and respect of a father: "One time he took my hand
and said to me, 'You poor, poor girl, I'll pray for you!'"

And it was to her the prisoner gave his poor set of rosary

beads, made of wire and wood, and when she snapped that the thing would do her no good because she did not know how to pray, Titus said to her, "You don't have to say the whole Hail Mary. Just say, 'Pray for us sinners.'"

And it was to her that, on that July 25, 1942, the doctor of the ward gave the syringe of carbolic acid with which to inject him. It was a *routine* chore, one the nurse had already done hundreds and hundreds of times, but the poor woman would recall later that she "felt sick that whole day". The injection was given at ten minutes to two, and at two o'clock Titus died. "I was there when he breathed his last. . . . The doctor was sitting next to the bed with a stethoscope to keep up appearances. When the heart stopped beating, he said to me, 'This pig is dead!'"

Father Titus had always said about his torturers, "They, too, are children of the good God, and perhaps there is still something left in them. . . ."

And God granted him precisely this last miracle. The camp doctor sarcastically called that shot of poison the "injection of grace". And, indeed, as the nurse was injecting him, it was the intercession of Titus that truly infused into her the grace of God. And the poor woman, during the canonical investigation, explained that the face of that elderly priest had remained stamped in her memory forever, because she had read something there that she had never known before. She simply said, "He had compassion for me."

Like Christ.

In this way, with the tenderness of a humiliated father, Brandsma was able to bring to life the one who had just given him death.

Saint Oscar Romero
(1917–1980)

Appointed in 1977 as archbishop of San Salvador, capital of the South American republic of El Salvador, Oscar Romero[6] had a reputation for keeping to himself and being more inclined to study than to struggles and social conflict. But over the course of his impassioned episcopal ministry, seeing up close the sufferings of his people, who were oppressed by an unjust and violent dictatorship and shaken by the example of some of his fellow clerics who were persecuted and killed by the regime, he became a "good shepherd" and a combative one, ready to give his life in defense of his flock. He began to condemn the crimes of the state publicly in his Sunday homilies, and his preaching was broadcast on the radio in his country and even abroad. After months and months of passion and of courageous resistance, one Sunday he directly addressed the soldiers, asking them to stop killing in the name of the dictators and of the rich landowners:

> I would like to make an appeal in a special way to the men of the army. . . . Brothers, you are part of our own people. You kill your own campesino brothers and sisters. And before an order that a man may give to kill, the law of God must prevail that says: Thou shalt not kill! No soldier is obliged to obey an order against the law of God. No one has to fulfill an immoral law. It is time to recover your consciences and obey your consciences rather than the orders of sin. The Church, defender of the rights of God, of the law of God, of human dignity, the dignity of the person, cannot remain silent before such an abomination. In the name of God, and in the name of this suffer-

---

[6] Beatified on May 23, 2015, Oscar Romero has subsequently been recognized as a saint, having been canonized on October 14, 2018.—ED.

ing people whose laments rise to heaven each day more tu-
multuously, I beg you, I ask you, I order you in the name
of God: Stop the repression![7]

With these words, Romero had signed his death warrant,
and deep in his heart he knew it.

On the afternoon of the following day, Monday, March
24, 1980, Romero celebrated Mass in the chapel of the *hos-
pitalito*, the hospital of Divine Providence for terminal cancer patients (where he had decided to live, in three little
rooms originally intended for the janitor). In his homily, he
commented on the Gospel of the grain of wheat, which in
falling to the ground must die in order to bear fruit.

Then he applied this to the Eucharist he was about to
offer:

> At this moment, the wheaten host is changed into the body
> of the Lord, who offered himself for the world's redemp-
> tion, and in this chalice the wine is transformed into the
> blood that was the price of salvation. May this body im-
> molated and this blood sacrificed for humans nourish us
> also, so that we may give our body and blood to suffering
> and to pain—like Christ, not for self, but to teach justice
> and peace to our people. Let us join together intimately in
> faith and hope at this moment of prayer.[8]

Then he went to the altar and turned toward the people
to begin the Offertory. From the back of the church there
was a gunshot. The frightened faithful dove to the floor.
When they got back up, they saw their archbishop lying beside the altar, hit with a bullet that had fragmented inside his
chest. Falling with his hands still holding on to the corporal,

---

[7] As quoted in: Christian Smith, *The Emergence of Liberation Theology*
(Chicago and London: Univ. of Chicago Press, 1991), p. 2.

[8] As quoted in: James R. Brockman, *Romero: A Life* (New York: Orbis
Books, 2005), p. 241.

Romero had pulled the wine onto his body along with the hosts he was to consecrate, which were all soaked in his blood.

The martyrdom continued the following Sunday, during his funeral, when the ceremony was violently interrupted with gunshots that sowed panic amid the huge crowd, and when it was all over, there were forty corpses on the ground, people trampled in the crush.

So Archbishop Romero died replacing the hosts and wine he was to consecrate with his own body and blood.

All the martyrs mingle their blood with that of Jesus: they die by His death and rise again through His life. But those who die physically embracing the Eucharist, almost clasping it to their hearts, or even while celebrating the Eucharistic Sacrifice, are among the privileged.

Becoming Eucharist for one's brothers, in fact, is the task assigned to all Christians, but doing so with the physical elements is the extraordinary gift that the whole Church received from Archbishop Romero.

Blessed Giuseppe "Pino" Puglisi
(1937–1993)

He is the tenth and last martyr we wish to recall, emphasizing also the unusual character of his martyrdom: that of a parish priest in the midst of his people, killed while trying to keep his boys away from the organized crime that runs rampant in the place he was from.

Ordained a priest at the age of twenty-three, Father Puglisi was first a chaplain and parish priest, then a religion teacher at various schools and a spiritual director at the diocesan seminary.

In 1990, he was appointed pastor of his childhood parish, in a neighborhood on the outskirts of Palermo, where the Mafia trained boys to become its future foot soldiers. Father Pino stood up to the Mafia and defended his "street kids", offering them an educational center that he named *Padre nostro*. At the same time, he spoke out against the graft and extortion that were devastating the neighborhood and the parish.

When—after many threats and intimidations—the Mafia decided to get him out of the way, Father Pino was so defenseless the job was a breeze. It was the day of his fifty-sixth birthday. In the morning, he had celebrated two weddings, after which he had gone into town for his latest fruitless attempt to get a middle school off the ground. In the afternoon, he had met up with some friends for a little celebration and a birthday card; then he had prepared several parents for the baptism of their children, after which he was heading home for one last meeting with a married couple who wanted to talk with him. The hit men were shadowing him, but only to size up the job, study the situation. And the situation was so simple (and the victim so exposed!), they figured there was no reason to wait. While Father Pino was fitting his key into the gate outside his home, a hand stopped him and reached for his satchel, "Father, this is a robbery", said the perpetrator.

Father Pino just barely turned toward him.

"I was expecting this", he said with an unforgettable kindly smile as the hit man shot him in the back of the head. He was *expecting* to give his life at that very moment? We do not know, because he did not see his killer and perhaps felt only a vaguely menacing presence behind him.

During those last years—although he was pastor in Brancaccio and a spiritual director at the seminary—he had not wanted to abandon a post he held dear, that of chaplain of a shelter for teenage mothers. The day before, he had delivered to those young women a very strange homily on the Passion of Jesus. He had said:

> When we are afraid or feel an intense sensation of heat, contractions break out below the skin. Underneath there are things like little sacks that empty themselves and make the sweat come out. But when the contraction is stronger, because the fear has become anguish, unbearable tension, the capillaries break. This is why it is said that Christ sweated blood. . . . He sweated blood on account of the human fear of pain. . . . He pleaded with the Father to take the bitter cup away, before uniting Himself with His will. All of this makes us feel that Christ is even closer to us, like a brother. He gave His life for us, and we too should give our lives for our brothers.

Now we know what Father Puglisi was waiting for: he was waiting for the moment in which Christ crucified would embrace him and clasp him to Himself.

~

And many other everyday martyrs

This last martyrdom we have recounted could be defined as "a poor martyrdom" (also like the Eucharist, which is bread humbly broken that can be consumed every day), prepared and tasted slowly, as Jesus tasted it along the unstoppable journey that would lead Him first to Jerusalem and then to Golgotha. This was how Father Pino Puglisi walked along the streets of his neighborhood that were ruled by the Mafia, taking an interest in all the problems of the people, accom-

panying his laity with true and active pastoral charity, defending and supporting all just causes, and knowing that
for him all the streets had become a long Via Crucis upon
which he had freely set out: he knew any form of violence
that might come his way was a sacred station of his journey
toward Calvary. But in the end, he too found the arms of
Jesus holding him up.

And these atypical experiences of long martyrdom, like
the one lived by Father Puglisi—portioned out over all the
hours of many days—remind us that today, amid the re-
sumption of the bloody ancient persecutions with the same
ancient ferocity of the first centuries, Christians can be persecuted not only in extreme forms that demand the explicit
and courageous testimony given in a supreme and conclusive act but also in monotonous and ongoing forms.

They are persecutions that unfold over days and days of
growing hostility, of systematic manipulation, of threats that
are certain even if they are not clearly defined.

Methodical aggression may be applied to the Christian's
faith, his charity, his hunger and thirst for justice, his passion for the truth, his affection for the Church.

And the martyrdom can take a thousand forms, which can
even be anonymous: at times the martyr is an indistinct face
among hundreds of other equally disfigured faces; at times
the martyrdom is hidden in an apparently random death that
was, however, planned or even just hinted at by the persecutors; at times the martyr's "yes" to Christ is hidden in
the "no" that he says to the violent of this world.

Back in the early 1950s, the well-known theologian
Charles Journet warned: "It may be that the era we have
entered will bring a form of martyrdom that is very poor,
very bare, without anything spectacular for the faith of the
Christian community—given that everything spectacular is

going on in the camp of the Beast—an era in which the martyrs will be asked, before dying bodily for Christ, to be disheartened and to give up even the joy of being able to confess Jesus before the world."

Today the two forms of vocation to martyrdom (extreme and everyday) seem to be interwoven, both becoming customary.

CHAPTER II

Dying of Love

How broad God's communality!
He teacheth whomso'er He list,
The peasant lass no less than thee,
The art whereby He may be kissed.

Thus sings the mystical poet Angelus Silesius in *The Cherubinic Wanderer.*[1]

In the history of Christianity, it has been above all the martyrs who have experienced and taught to what extent the identification of the faithful with Christ should be driven. But paradigmatic among these are several enamored young women who gave their lives to Him with a nuptial sensibility.

The names of Agatha, Lucy, Agnes, Cecilia, and Anastasia are still celebrated in the *Roman Canon.*

Particularly vivid is the memory of Saint Agnes' loving witness, preserved by the bishop Saint Ambrose: "What allurements to persuade her, how many desired that she would come to them in marriage! But she answered: 'It would be an injury to my spouse to look on any one as likely to please me. He who chose me first for Himself shall receive me.'"[2]

---

[1] Selections from Angelus Silesius, *The Cherubinic Wanderer*, trans. with an introduction by J. E. Crawford Flitch (London: Allen & Unwin, 1932).

[2] St. Ambrose, *Concerning Virgins*, trans. H. de Romestin, bk. 1, chap. 2, no. 9, in *Nicene and Post-Nicene Fathers*, Second Series, vol. 10, ed. Philip Schaff and Henry Wace (1896; Peabody, Mass.: Hendrickson, 1995), p. 364. *PL* 16:189–91.

This was why, over the course of the centuries, once the era of persecutions was over, Christians took as their ideal image those who chose to consecrate themselves to Christ in the state of virginity, thus following him "more closely".

This falling in love with Jesus was not, however, a privilege for women alone, because the deepest and unique identity of every baptized person (before, during, after, and also without marriage)—and, indeed, the deepest and unique identity of every human creature—consists in the fact that each one belongs always, personally and amorously, to Christ the Bridegroom.

And there is a certain spiritual depth at which the being, whether male or female, no longer poses any difficulty over the fact of falling in love with Christ in a spousal sense.

So we would like to begin by evoking the paradigmatic falling in love of two saints, Francis of Assisi and John of the Cross, who, on the one hand, experienced a true and profound spousal relationship with Christ, almost embodying the Church as Bride, and, on the other—precisely because of this—became ever more like Him.

Saint Francis of Assisi
(1181–1226)

The example of Saint Francis of Assisi is the best known and the most fascinating. His first biographer, Thomas of Celano, writes: "The friars who lived with him know very well how every day, or rather every moment, the recollection of Christ blossomed from his lips, with what warmth and sweetness he spoke with Him, with what tender love he conversed with Him. He was indeed greatly occupied with Jesus. He carried always Jesus in his heart, Jesus on his lips,

Jesus in his ears, Jesus in his eyes, Jesus in his hands, Jesus in all his other members."[3]

And he is not afraid to describe some of his typically spousal outpourings: "When the saint prayed, in the forests and in solitary places, he filled the woods with sobs, bathed the ground with tears, beat his breast with his hand; and there, taking advantage, as it were, of that more intimate and secluded place, he often conversed aloud with his Lord, rendered an account to the Judge, pleaded with the Father, spoke with the Friend, joked amiably with the Bridegroom."[4]

Also particularly characteristic in the saint of Assisi was the phenomenon of the stigmata (a miracle that had never happened before!), sign of a love so intense that after impregnating the soul, it overflows into the body as well.

A phenomenon that Saint Francis de Sales, in his *Treatise on the Love of God*, explains like this:

Ah! how much more extreme was the tenderness of the great St. Francis when he saw the picture of our Lord as he sacrificed himself on the cross! . . . [This] soul was so softened, made tender, and almost dissolved in this amorous pain that he was completely disposed to receive the impressions and marks of his supreme lover's love and sorrow. His memory was wholly steeped in remembrance of that divine love. His imagination was forcibly employed to represent to him the wounds and bruises his eyes saw so perfectly expressed in the image before him. His intellect received those most vivid forms which his imagination furnished to it. Finally, love made use of all the powers of his will to enter into the passion of his beloved and conform to it. Hence beyond doubt his soul

---

[3] *Vita prima*, no. 115.
[4] *Vita seconda*, LXI, 95.

was transformed completely into a second Crucified. As the body's form and master, the soul exercised its authority over the body and stamped the pain of the wounds it endured on the parts corresponding to those where its beloved had suffered them. Love has a wonderful power to sharpen the imagination so that it can penetrate beyond itself. . . . Love drove the interior torment of so great a lover as St. Francis to his exterior person. It wounded his body with that same dart of pain with which it had wounded his soul. [5]

And there is certainly a wealth of ecclesial symbolism in what happened upon the death of the saint, when the funeral procession stopped at San Damiano and the casket was opened so that Saint Clare and her "poor women" could kiss his stigmata.

Saint John of the Cross
(1542–1591)

The example of Saint John of the Cross is not as well known in terms of popular awareness, but it is even more decisive in terms of his teaching as Doctor of the Church.

At a crucial time in Christian history, he in fact had the mission of "saving" and bringing back to the center of theological and spiritual reflection the biblical *Song of Songs*.

Until the sixteenth century, theological reflection had been based on the various commentaries on the *Song* offered by the Fathers of the Church or by other spiritual writers.

But with the crisis provoked by the Protestant Reforma-

---

[5] St. Francis de Sales, *Treatise on the Love of God*, vol. 1, trans. John K. Ryan (Rockford, Ill.: TAN Books, 1975), bk. VI, chap. 15, pp. 312–13.

tion, it seemed everything had to be limited to ever more rigid reflections on faith, at the expense of love and charity.

In those years of great upheaval, Christian mysticism would have been seriously wounded and impoverished if John of the Cross had not received the gift of reinterpreting the biblical text of the *Song*, almost rewriting it with renewed poetic inspiration in the forty stanzas of his *Spiritual Canticle*, after which he gave it a trinitarian fulfillment in the *Living Flame of Love* and, finally, commented theologically on his own poems.

Saint John of the Cross was, therefore, the *teacher in the faith*[6] who had the gift and the task of speaking once again to the Church-as-Bride—with fitting beauty—the biblical word that "the most sweet Jesus, Bridegroom of faithful souls"[7] addresses to them: a word that is entirely a dialogue of love.

So it is not without significance that this saint (considered the greatest love poet in the Spanish language) died while listening once again to those divine words that are the heart of Sacred Scripture.

We know that when his fellow friars gathered around his cot and started to recite the prayers for the dying, the saint interrupted them, saying to his superior, "Father, I do not need this, read me something from the *Song of Songs*."

And as those verses of love resounded in the cell, John sighed with delight, "What precious pearls!"

At midnight, when the bells were ringing for Matins, he exclaimed, "Glory to God, I am going to sing it in heaven!"

---

[6] Pope St. John Paul II, Apostolic letter of December 14, 1990.

[7] *The Spiritual Canticle*, 40, 7, in *The Collected Works of St. John of the Cross*, trans. Kieran Kavanaugh, O.C.D., and Otilio Rodriguez, O.C.D., 3rd ed. (Washington, D.C.: ICS Publications; Institute of Carmelite Studies, 2017), p. 630.

Then he looked right at each of those present as if saying goodbye, kissed the crucifix, and said, "Lord, into your hands I commend my spirit!"

So he died in Ubeda on December 14, 1591, and those present recounted that a gentle light and an intense perfume had filled the cell, just as before they had filled his gloomy prison in Toledo, becoming images, aromas, and sounds worthy of an amorous human-divine tableau.

On the one hand, therefore, Saint Francis of Assisi and Saint John of the Cross with their attitude reminded us of the attitudes of the believing soul as Bride of Christ, while, on the other hand, with their teaching they also evoked the image of Christ the Bridegroom.

Now, however, we would like to study the faces of several "enamored virgins", selecting, above all, the holy women who dedicated themselves to a contemplative life, setting themselves, so to speak, "in defense of the heart".

With this last expression, we would like to emphasize the need never to trivialize holiness by making it a purely moral or sociological question.

Holy men and women are, in fact, often evaluated historically by what they have been able to achieve through their teaching, enterprise, and apostolic action, leaving shrouded in shadows the most valuable part of their experience, which is their relationship with the Divine Persons.

It seems to many that they would still be significant and exemplary figures on account of their works, even without Christ: even if they had not had (better: even if they *did not have*, since they are all *living* persons) a Christ to love and a Christ who loves them.

But this would leave the saints without their hearts!

That is why God also gives the Church virginal and contemplative figures who are not distinguished by the works they do but whose only aim in life seems to be that of letting Him love them and loving Him with every fiber of their being.

The evangelical image of the *precious perfume*, poured out for no other reason than to honor the beloved body of Christ —while someone yells about the waste[8]—describes fairly well the gift and task included in their spiritual experience.

[8] Cf. Jn 12:1–8. This is how St. Thérèse of Lisieux (of whom we shall speak shortly) defended in a letter the importance and beauty of her cloistered vocation:

What a joy to suffer for Him who loves us unto *folly*, and to pass as *fools* in the eyes of the world. We judge others as we judge ourselves, and since the world is senseless, it naturally thinks we are the ones who are senseless! . . . But, after all, we are not the first; the only crime with which Jesus was reproached by Herod was that of being *foolish*, and I think like him! . . . Yes, indeed, it was *folly* to seek out the poor little hearts of mortals to make them His *thrones*, He, the King of Glory, who is seated above the Cherubim . . . He, whom the heavens cannot contain. . . . He was *foolish*, our Beloved, to come to earth in search of sinners in order to make them His friends, His intimates, His *equals*, He, who was perfectly happy with the two adorable Persons of the Trinity! . . . We shall never be able to carry out the follies He carried out for us, and our action will never merit this name, for they are only very rational acts and much below what our love would like to accomplish. It is the world, then, that is senseless since it does not know what Jesus has done to save it, it is the world which is a *monopolizer*, which seduces souls, and which leads them to springs without water. . . .

We are not *idlers*, squanderers, either. Jesus has defended us in the person of the Magdalene. He was at table, Martha was serving, Lazarus was eating with Him and His disciples. As for Mary, she was not thinking of taking any food but of *pleasing* Him whom she loved, so she took a jar filled with an ointment of great price and poured it on the *head* of Jesus, after *breaking the jar*, and the whole house was scented with the ointment, but the APOS-TLES *complained* against Magdalene. . . . It is really the same for us, the most fervent *Christians, priests*, find that we are *exaggerated*, that we should *serve* with Martha instead of consecrating to Jesus the *vessels* of our *lives*, with the ointment enclosed within them. . . . And nevertheless what does it matter if our *vessels* be broken since Jesus is *consoled* and since, in spite of itself, the world is obliged *to smell* the perfumes that are exhaled and serve to purify the empoisoned air the world never ceases to breathe in.

LT 169, August 19, 1894, from Thérèse to Céline, in St. Thérèse of Lisieux, *General Correspondence*, vol. 2, trans. John Clarke, O.C.D. (Washington, D.C.: Institute of Carmelite Studies, 1988), pp. 882–83.

And when the jar that contains such a precious perfume is shattered (at the moment of death), it is love that overflows from all the wounds.

So right away let us place around Saint John of the Cross several young "Carmelite brides" who—from him and from Saint Teresa of Ávila[9]—learned to realize in the first place their own spiritual marriage with Christ.

Saint Teresa Margaret of the Sacred Heart
(1747–1770)

She was very young when she entered the Carmelite monastery in Florence, where the majority of the nuns were elderly. Although she had chosen a cloistered form of life, she found herself acting as nurse for all the others, living her contemplative vocation by incorporating within herself love of God and love of neighbor (the two loves that are united in the person of Jesus, our God and our neighbor).

Her fidelity to her vocation received decisive support from the fact that since childhood she had cultivated an intense devotion to the Heart of Jesus (which was rare for those times). So she had set for herself as her only ideal that of "giving back to him love for love". She used to say, "He on the cross for me, and I on the cross for Him!" She had read in Scripture that "God is love" and had got lost, as it were, in that ocean, from which she never wanted to emerge. All she needed was to give herself without rest and without complaint to her sick fellow Sisters.

And when she was the one who fell gravely ill, almost no-

[9] We will speak of the great Teresa later, placing her on the next list, that of the great Mothers who gave their lives to build up the Church and to provide for the Bridegroom a worthy Dwelling.

body noticed. The doctor who was called for her shrugged it off, saying it was "an illness of little consequence". In reality, it was peritonitis, and gangrene had already set in. So Sister Teresa Margaret died on her cot, trying to keep herself facing the chapel of the Most Holy Sacrament and pressing to her chest an image of the Sacred Heart.

After the funeral, her body was placed in a damp cellar to await burial, but no one had the courage to bury it, since with every hour that went by, it seemed to acquire new youthful freshness, and an unexpected perfume had pervaded the crypt. The body is still incorrupt today. Teresa Margaret had cared for so many suffering members, with such tenderness, that Jesus had used the same tenderness even for her earthly body.

Saint Mary of Jesus Crucified
(1846–1878)

Alongside her it is nice to be able to place right away Saint *Mariam Baouardy*, perhaps the least known Carmelite nun, but also one canonized recently (2015). Her religious name is *Mary of Jesus Crucified*.

Born in Galilee to an Arab Catholic family, she belongs to all three of those peoples of the East that are still fighting it out in the land of Jesus and are in need of peace. And this is why there is consolation in knowing that today, in the village where she was born, she is also venerated by the non-Christians.

Mariam spent her life between Palestine, Syria, France, and India, finally returning to Palestine to found the Carmelite monastery of Bethlehem. Wherever she went, she was seen as "a miracle of God's grace", but she always looked on herself as "a little nobody". She wanted only to be "the little Arab", as everyone called her on account of her minuscule stature. She said: "The thought that I am a nobody makes me jump for joy. It is so beautiful to be a nobody. . . . Humility is happy to be a nobody, is not attached to anything, never gets upset. It is content, happy, everywhere happy, satisfied with everything. . . . Blessed are the lowly."

And yet God had given her a *"wonderful life"*: an existence entirely steeped in miracles and extraordinary wonders, so much so that her first biography—published in France with the title *Golden Legend Beyond the Sea*—was stirring and enchanting for famous intellectuals like Léon Bloy, Jacques Maritain, and Julien Green.

Illiterate, she composed by memory beautiful poems that sounded like Psalms. One of them says:

> "What do I resemble, Lord?
> The unfledged little birds in their nest.
> If the father and mother do not bring them food
> they die of hunger.
> So is my soul
> without you, O Lord.
> It has no sustenance, it cannot live."

Death took her, at the age of thirty-three, while she was toiling at the foundation of a second monastery in Nazareth. She said she felt increasingly drawn to God, "hounded more and more by love". She prayed: "I cannot live any longer, O God, I cannot live any longer. Call me to you!"

That August, 1878—while she was heading down a steep garden path with two pails of water for some thirsty brick-layers—she fell over a planter of geraniums and broke her arm in several places between the wrist and elbow. By the next day, she had already developed gangrene. She then said happily, "I am on the way to heaven. I am about to go to Jesus."

She suffered all day long, but she kept repeating, "Come, Lord Jesus, come!"

At five o'clock the next morning, it seemed she could not breathe. The community was called. They had a last prayer to suggest for her:

"My Jesus, Mercy!"

She repeated:

"Yes, mercy!"

And she died kissing the crucifix.

Today her tomb is a pilgrimage destination for Christians and Muslims.

Saint Thérèse of Lisieux
(1873–1897)

She was five years old when the little Arab died. And without knowing it, she was inheriting the same language and the same passion for being and feeling small before God. With her account of the graces she received in her family, already during her childhood years (an account enriched with many spiritual reflections), Thérèse would become "the most beloved girl on earth", and today she is universally known as "the teacher of spiritual childhood".

It must, however, be pointed out that this was not a matter of a spiritualization or poetic idealization of the age of childhood, but an ecclesial assimilation of the childhood of Jesus, who remained always the "Child of the Father", from crib to Cross.

The childhood that Thérèse always desired and cultivated was, therefore, what situated her in the heart of the Church, where love is stored up and overflows, spreading through missionary activity to the ends of the earth. So this was not a matter of "being" or "remaining" a child, but of "becoming" one (as the Gospel teaches) by learning from Jesus.

This is why, as a Carmelite nun, Thérèse, looking at the difficult sufferings of her elderly father (in whom she recognized "the child of God") and realizing God was in a hurry to call her to Himself, understood one of her most important tasks would be that of "learning to die", and the sufferings necessary for that extraordinary maturation would not be in short supply.

From the theological point of view, the account of Thérèse's death—which is not very widely known—has something extraordinary about it and is worth exploring in its entirety.[10] We can affirm that it contains one of the most beautiful pages of her teaching.

Thérèse, then, became gravely ill with tuberculosis one year before she died. During her last illness, she said at times: "What must I do to die? Never will I know how to die!"

She intuited that her trial would be terrible: her body was rapidly wearing down, and the illness was giving her intolerable pains. Her lungs were completely devastated, and it was extremely difficult for her to breathe, at a time when giving her oxygen was not even a possibility. Her breathing itself seemed to reproduce the first efforts of the child just seeing the light of day. This frightened her, "If I can't breathe, God will give me the strength to bear it." "At each breath I suffer violently. But not to the point of crying out."

And speaking to Mother Agnes of Jesus: "Mamma! . . . earth's air is denied to me, when will God grant me the air of heaven?"

Her last months were marked by a suffering that spread

[10] Cf. St. Thérèse of Lisieux, *Her Last Conversations*, trans. John Clarke, O.C.D. (Washington, D.C.: ICS Publications; Institute of Carmelite Studies, 1977).

itself ever more like a sea surrounding her on all sides and asking of her—this time completely—the abandonment of a sick child who has to rely on everyone:

"Last night I couldn't take anymore; I asked the Blessed Virgin to hold my head in her hands so that I could take my sufferings." "I forgot self, and I was careful to seek myself in nothing." "I'm suffering only for an instant." "Little children are not damned." "As far as little ones are concerned, they will be judged with great gentleness. And one can remain little, even in the most formidable offices, even when living for a long time. If I were to die at the age of eighty, . . . I would still die, I feel, as little as I am today."

To those who asked her if her sufferings had become unbearable, she replied, "No, it still allows me to tell God that I love Him; and I find that this is enough. . . . I love everything that God gives me."

But if anyone praised her for her great patience, she answered like someone who feels she is not yet understood, "I haven't even one minute of patience. It's not my patience! . . . You're always wrong!"

She maintained the same way of expressing herself and her comparisons with childhood, in spite of the fact that she was immersed in unspeakable sufferings. She recounted to her sisters, "The first time I was given grapes in the infirmary, I said to Jesus: How good the grapes are! I can't understand why You are waiting so long to take me, since I too am a little grape, and they tell me I'm so ripe!"

One day, when it she seemed she was dozing, one of her sisters who asked about her at the door of the infirmary was told, "She is very tired!"

Thérèse heard this and later recounted, "I was thinking: That's really true, I am! Yes, I'm like a tired and harassed traveller, who reaches the end of his journey and falls over. Yes, but I'll be falling into God's arms."

And that is just what happened to her. She had a long and excruciating death agony. Her sister recounts: "A terrible rattle tore her chest. Her face was blue, her hands purplish, her feet were cold, and she shook in all her members. . . ." This lasted a few hours. Toward the evening she looked at her prioress and said, "Mother, isn't this the agony! . . . Am I not going to die?" The prioress answered that "'God perhaps wills to prolong it for several hours.' She answered with courage: 'Well . . . All right! . . . All right Oh! I would not want to suffer for a shorter time! . . .' And looking at her Crucifix: 'Oh! I love Him! My God . . . I love you!'"[11] Her head fell backward, her eyes remained fixed for the duration of a Credo, dazzling. Then she expired.

In dying with that perfectly simple and all-encompassing expression on her lips ("My God, I love you!") the little Thérèse has remained the clearest icon of the one who "dies of love" because by love she *lives*: an experience she had already selected as the title and refrain of a little poem (*Living on Love*) into which she had poured all her desires for holiness.

Saint Elizabeth of the Trinity
(1880–1906)

From the beautiful theological analysis Hans Urs von Balthasar has bequeathed to us,[12] we know Elizabeth was a "sister in the spirit" of Saint Thérèse of Lisieux.

[11] St. Thérèse of Lisieux, *Her Last Conversations*, trans. John Clarke, O.C.D. (Washington, C.D.: ICS Publications, Institute of Carmelite Studies, 1977), p. 206.

[12] Hans Urs von Balthasar, *Two Sisters in the Spirit: Thérèse of Lisieux and Elizabeth of the Trinity*, trans. Donald Nichols et al. (San Francisco: Ignatius Press, 1992). (Beatified on November 25, 1984, Elizabeth of the Trinity was subsequently recognized as a saint and canonized on October 16, 2016.— ED.)

It is together that one must listen to them in order to perceive all the registers of Carmelite sanctity.

So if Thérèse was hidden in the heart of the Church (and from there her intercession and her teaching have circulated to the ends of the earth), Elizabeth was entirely enclosed within the bosom of the Trinity, "still" and "peaceful" in order to offer herself for a "kind of incarnation of the Word".[13]

Inhabiting God-as-Trinity and *being inhabited* was her irresistible vocation.

But for her as well there came the time—as for Thérèse, although in a different way—to learn the immense depths that are opened up when Christ asks the soul to accompany Him in his Passion.

At the age of twenty-five, Elizabeth was struck with one of the most terrible illnesses, Addison's disease, which was incurable at the time. This is a serious disorder of the adrenal glands above the kidneys, which no longer produce the substances necessary for metabolism. With it came food intolerance, crises of hunger, serious dehydration, insomnia, nausea, unbearable headaches . . . She was not spared anything: not even the temptation of suicide.

So it seemed that even before she got sick, Elizabeth already knew all the depths of the mystery of God, as young as she was; and yet there was still something she lacked. She lacked the experience of suffering. And one cannot truly know the love of Christ if one does not know the blood price He paid for us. This is why during the last months of her life, Elizabeth continually repeated an expression that also figures as a refrain in her last letters: "Where did Christ dwell, if not in suffering?"

---

[13] "O My God, Trinity Whom I Adore", a prayer of Elizabeth of the Trinity, in her *Complete Works*, vol. 1, trans. Sister Aletheia Kane, O.C.D. (Washington, D.C.: ICS Publications, 1984), pp. 183–91.

That is what the famous medieval mystic Saint Angela of Foligno used to say and teach, and Elizabeth used it to remember that only when one enters into the Passion of Christ does one truly meet Him "at home" and get to know Him.

This brought to completion the journey little Elizabeth had begun on the day of her First Communion. At the time, she had said her name meant "house of God", and becoming this was her vocation. Now she understood she had to bear within herself the image of the crucified God, to the point of being conformed to Him.

In this way she lived her last months. She said:

"When I lie down on my little bed, I imagine I am climbing onto my altar, and I say to Him, 'My God, do not hesitate!' Sometimes anguish comes, but then I very quietly calm down and tell Him: 'My God, this doesn't count'". . . .[14]

She wrote in one of her last letters: "On my cross where I taste unknown joys, I understand that suffering is the revelation of Love, and I rush to it: it is my beloved dwelling place where I find peace and rest, here where I am sure to meet my Master" (Letter 323).[15]

But there is something else decisive that has to be added: this last agonizing "heart to heart with Jesus" did not isolate Elizabeth from her affections and responsibilities.

She knew there was still something unresolved with her mother, who had resisted her daughter's departure for the monastery and had kept her from realizing her vocation until she reached adulthood.

Now that Elizabeth was dying, God was about to ask her mother for a final and more serious detachment, and the

[14] Elizabeth of the Trinity, *The Complete Works*, vol. 2, trans. Anne Englund Nash (Washington, D.C.: ICS Publications, Institute of Carmelite Studies, 1995), L 306, p. 320n1.

[15] Ibid., p. 344.

daughter decided this time she would pull her mother along in the very act of offering herself.

She did so at their last meeting, through the parlor grate. Here is the account her mother left for us: "By this time all the life she had left was concentrated in her eyes. And at the end of that last meeting, she had the courage to say to me, 'Mother, when the nun comes to notify you that I have stopped suffering, you must fall to your knees and say: "My God, You gave her to me and I give her back to you. Blessed be your holy Name!"'"

And we know that afterward, she obeyed, repeating word for word the offering her daughter had put on her lips and in her heart.

This, too, is dying as enamored saints: going to God with a direct movement, without turning aside, but gathering up and bringing along all the creatures He has entrusted to us.

Saint Teresa of the Andes
(1900–1920)

After the death of little Thérèse of Lisieux (1897) and before the death of Elizabeth of Dijon (1906), Chile saw the birth of Juana Fernández Solar, who would become Teresa of the Andes, the first non-European Carmelite woman to be proclaimed a saint.

From a prosperous family, she lived her young years to the full, always showing herself to be cheerful, simple, charming, athletic, forthright, although she was often plagued with health problems. But it was precisely these sufferings that became the secret between her and Jesus, to whom Juana had given her heart from the day of her first Communion.

She entered the monastery at the age of nineteen but did

not even make it through the novitiate. And yet among all the Carmelite saints, none other than she (the youngest!) was entrusted with the most difficult mission: that of proclaiming that love and suffering are inseparable.

No Carmelite saint knew the simple joys of the world, of nature, of family, of youth, of friendship, of sports like Juana. And none suffered like she did during her childhood, adolescence, and young adulthood.

But along with her experience, she has also left us these burning questions: How is it possible to fall in love with one crucified without caring about His pains, His concerns, His wounds, His abandonment, His sacrifice, His Eucharistic self-giving?

And already at the beginning of her first Lent in the monastery, Teresa knew within herself she would have to give Him everything. Here is a poem she wrote at the time:

> "I begin to walk
> in order to die on the Cross. . . .
> What does it matter, when one loves,
> to carry a heavy cross,
> if one burns with a holy flame?
> What can the heart desire
> after it has tasted the sweetness of Your love?"

She showed this by dying, not of pain, but of "passion" (the same as that of Christ) and of love.

The crisis began on Holy Thursday of 1920. She had a very high fever, and even though at least six doctors took turns at her sickbed, they were not able to diagnose in time that what she had was typhus.

She received extreme unction, and, to make her dream come true, the prioress allowed her to make her religious vows *in articulo mortis*, even though she had not yet completed the novitiate. So Juana, who became Sister Teresa of Jesus, made her profession and was so happy about it she wanted to repeat the formula three times, even though she no longer had even enough strength to sign the document she had just read.

On the evening of the Friday after Easter, the sick woman showed she was in the grip of great anguish, as if she were again shrouded in the darkness of Calvary and again assailed by the temptation to despair. She felt abandoned by heaven and trembled with anguish at the thought of God's judgment. But this was what she herself had asked, in order to resemble her Crucified One to the very end.

Then came peace. The smile returned to her face, and her gaze settled on an exact spot, as if Someone had finally arrived. They heard her exclaim, thrilled as could be, "My Bridegroom!"

And when she died, her fellow Sisters had the impression "that she was immersed in an immense happiness".

Teresa de Los Andes was canonized by Saint John Paul II in 1993. And it is significant that, in an outer niche of the apse of Saint Peter's Basilica in the Vatican, a statue has been placed that was carved from a single block of Carrara marble by a great-nephew of the saint. And the sculptor gave his work this splendid title, so suited to the theme we are exploring: *L'Innamorata*.

Blessed Maria Candida of the Eucharist
(1884–1949)

She entered the Sicilian monastery of Ragusa at the age of thirty-five, in 1919 (the very same year in which the young Juana entered the Chilean monastery of Los Andes), living

the Carmelite vocation with a unique new spousal empha-
sis: that of impetuous love for Jesus-as-Eucharist.

The tabernacle was for Maria Candida the "seventh dwelling" of the *Interior Castle*, as described by Saint Teresa of
Ávila, and in the world she did not see beauty great enough
to deserve attention.

She wrote:

> Turning my gaze to all the beauty, all the greatness, all
> the splendors of the earth, and resting it again on the holy
> tabernacle, I feel, I exclaim that all is empty, that there is
> no treasure greater, more delicious, than that which I pos-
> sess, and that everything is right there! No, no one can
> possess more than I do, there is no other treasure: how
> rich and blessed I am! The divine treasure that is contained
> in the great basilicas, in the richly decorated tabernacles,
> is not greater than the one our humble little church pos-
> sesses, in our modest tabernacle! Heaven itself contains no
> more: that sole treasure is here, is mine, is God! Truly, yes,
> truly: *My God and my all!*

Therefore she prayed: "Jesus Eucharist, you have made
me for yourself, and I am all yours", and she paid him diligent attention every day by looking at and treating everything "with Eucharistic astonishment". She seemed never
able to satisfy herself, but such abundance was entirely contained in the perfectly simple formula with which she said,
"*my* Eucharist".

The Eucharist was the incarnation of Jesus, brought
within the reach of every heart and even of every human
body. She said: "In being born, Jesus became ours; in the
Eucharist, he makes Himself mine."

With this total dedication, in the end, all that was left
for her to do was to take a Eucharistic approach to meeting
death. She suffered a very long illness on account of a tumor

on her liver that brought her indescribable sufferings, but she insisted on saying it was all "a caress of infinite mercy" and that she "wanted to be immolated for Jesus with all happiness".

She died on the feast of the Most Holy Trinity in 1949. To her nuns she had said, "If on the point of death you see me weep, do not be amazed. I will be weeping for the great joy of going to heaven and for the tenderness that I feel in leaving you."

~

Let us now leave the "Carmelite garden" to contemplate other faces of brides of Christ, equally *enamored* but marked by another characteristic form of love: that of *a boundless humility*, that humility which Saint Teresa of Ávila also considered the "queen of virtues".

Saint Rita of Cascia
(1381–1457)

Hers is the first face we would like to recall, thinking back over all the vocations she had from God.

She was wife and mother; she had a violent husband and succeeded in converting him, but he was killed; she lost both her sons, who were in danger of being caught up in the ancestral feud, and she dedicated herself to bringing peace between the factions. Finally, she became an Augustinian nun, humble and hidden but loved by all.

The universal veneration that the Christian people bestowed upon her (which in time was confirmed by countless miracles) certainly originated in these various tragic experiences that Rita had to bear within her heart.

There is very little information about her monastic life, which she spent "in firmness and virtue". We are told only that "she persevered for forty years in serving God with love", without asking for anything except to bear at least some slight resemblance to her crucified Jesus. And she received the sacred sign of a thorn in her forehead. For many years, she remained gravely ill, surrounded on her poor pallet by the affection and veneration of the nuns and of all the people of Cascia. Near the end, she did not even have the strength (or perhaps the necessity) to nourish herself: she said that by then all she needed was the Eucharist. Her death was adorned with this episode that became a lovely part of her story:

> It therefore pleased God Our Lord to give an evident sign of the love that he bore for his cherished bride. In the bitter depths of winter, when everything was covered with snow, a kindly relative came to visit her; at parting, she asked her if she wanted anything from home. Rita replied that she would like a rose and two figs from her garden. The good woman smiled, believing that she was delirious on account of the severity of her illness, and she went on her way. When she got home and went to the garden for a different reason, she saw on top of the leafless, snow-covered thorns one exquisite rose and, on the tree, two ripe figs. Dumbfounded at seeing the miraculous flower and fruit in the frosty midwinter, she picked them and took them to Rita.

It was not just a miracle of courtesy but, rather, a mystical exchange: for many years, Rita had borne on her forehead the painful wound of the thorn; now, at the end of that passion, Christ was justly giving her a rose. When Rita died ("and immediately the bells of the monastery began

to ring of their own accord"), something certainly had to
happen to that holy body; there was the abundance of miracles given to those around it and the uninterrupted stream
of acquaintances and of the devout; there was an intense
perfume that emanated from it (a fact borne witness to repeatedly down to our own day); the body *was never buried
and has never become corrupt,* but is still exposed for veneration
in the fifteenth-century choir of the monastery.

Wherever there is a church dedicated to her, on the day
of her feast, May 22, her devotees flock to that place bearing
bouquets of roses.

Saint Josephine Bakhita
(1869–1947)

She was born in a remote African village in Darfur and was
kidnapped at the age of seven by a slave trader. After unspeakable sufferings, she was ransomed by the Italian am-
bassador, who had taken her into his service and brought
her with him to Venice. Entrusted to the Canossian Sisters,
Bakhita had asked to be baptized after learning to her amazement that she, too, was a child of God. She almost found this
hard to believe. Throughout the day, she would drop what
she was doing and run off to the catechist for reassurance:
really a daughter of God, she? Even though she was a slave?
Even though she was black? And He really loved her? Even
though she had nothing to give Him? She decided then that
God had always been and would always remain "her only
and true Master".

After she became a Canossian sister (with the help and
approval of the future Saint Pius X), they sent her to the

convent in Schio, where for the girls of the orphanage she became "Mother Moorette". She called them "my little mistresses".

She lived in the Schio convent for forty-two years: always very humble, obedient, happy.

As she got older, she could no longer move around on her own, and at times they left her in the chapel a bit too long, even two or three hours, huddled up in her wheelchair. When the nurse got there, out of breath and apologizing for having forgotten her, she replied contentedly in the Venetian dialect, "*Ah, mi me la son passà con Lu!*" (I spent my time with Him!)

She said it had been a gift, because she had got the chance to keep Jesus company. She said she was not tired; she felt good being there with the Lord . . . she would gladly stay with the Lord who had waited such a long time for her!

During her last months she added, "I'm leaving easy-does-it, step by step, because I have a heavy suitcase to carry!"

In reality, she had two heavy suitcases. And it is worthwhile to explain this strange image of hers. During the First World War, part of the convent had been designated as a military hospital, and Bakhita had often noticed that the captain's attendant always had to carry two suitcases: his own and that of his boss. That was it: she wanted to come before the eternal Father like a little soldier, carrying her suitcase and that of her Captain, Jesus. Then *el Paròn* (the Lord) would have her open the two suitcases: in her own, she would see many sins, but then, in the heavier one, she would see all the many, many merits of Jesus, and she would be welcomed with joy, because she had carried that suitcase, too!

In the delirium of her death agony, as if the past were coming back up from the "physical" depths of her memory, they heard her murmuring, "Take off the chains; they're heavy!"

The chains of slavery had become the chains of an overlong and wearisome life from which she wanted to be set free; and the humble request to unfasten the shackles had also become a prayer for obtaining the grace of the resurrection.

Her last words were, "How happy I am . . . Our Lady . . . Our Lady!"

So Bakhita entered into heaven, as a sister who intercedes before God for all the slaves of the earth.

Saint Maria Bertilla Boscardin
(1888–1922)

Born in the province of Vicenza to a family of illiterate peasants, she grew up timid and awkward, partly because of her father's harsh treatment. She was truly a *humiliated* creature, but she intuited by the grace of God that in a voluntary and holy way she could become *humble*. When she was fifteen, she told her confessor about her desire to consecrate herself to God, and she was accepted because of her candor and her willingness to learn.

"I am not good at anything, but I want to become a saint", she said, and specified: "a saint for heaven, not for the altar".

It was this desire that protected her from all self-absorption and left her willing to carry out any task assigned to her, no matter how humble and unsung. She was sent to the hospital in Treviso, where she worked in the kitchen for a whole year before being made the head of one of the most challenging wards (that of contagious children), when no one else could be found to do it. So she became a nurse at the age of twenty, showing tireless dedication. During the First World War, she was transferred to a hospital in Lombardy, where she had to face humiliation and disdain from a superior who was biased against her. Finally they sent her back to Treviso, where everyone fought over her, even though by this time she, too, was sick with a tumor. She died of it at the age of thirty-four, consumed by charity.

She was attended and observed, on her deathbed, by the chief physician (a freethinker and Freemason), who has left us an account of his own conversion, which took place in the presence of that "humble and enamored death" of a little nun who had given all of herself without demanding anything in return:

> I can affirm that the dawn of my spiritual transformation dates from watching Sister Bertilla as she was about to die. For her, in fact, whose hand I kissed shortly before she expired, dying was a joy plain for all to see. She died like no one I had ever seen die before, like someone who is already in a better state of life. . . . Oppressed by an extremely painful illness, bled dry, certain she was to die, in that state in which the patient ordinarily grabs on to the doctor and pleads 'save me', to hear her say with a smile I cannot describe, 'Be happy, Sisters, I am going to my God', was something that made me take a critical look at myself and that I now regard as the first miracle of Sister Bertilla. I said, in fact, to myself: This creature is as one beyond us, although she is alive. There is in her a material part that is still with us, giving thanks, comforting those around her; but there is also a spiritual part that is beyond, above us, much more evident and dominant: the spiritual part that already enjoys that happiness which was her breath of life.

What comes through in these reflections is the rationalist doctor confronted with evidence of the supernatural: one who has always denied the existence of the soul and is now almost forced to look at it as God takes it back to himself, and it jumps for joy to leave the body . . .

So the humble sister pulled along with her, in her faith, that intellectual proud of his science and of his free thinking, she who died with her dog-eared catechism in the pocket of her habit and who used to say: "I am a poor simpleton, but I believe all that the Church believes."

In a little notebook, she had delineated (with a few spelling mistakes that Jesus certainly did not mind at all) her program of life:

> I and God alone, inward and outward *recollection*, continual prayer, this is the air that I breathe; continual work, assiduous, but with calm and in good order. I am God's being, God has created me and preserves me, reason dictates that I should be all His. I seek happiness, but true happiness is found only in God. . . . I must do the will of Jesus without seeking anything, without wanting anything, with gladness, with good cheer. . . . *Supplicating* Jesus that He help me to overcome myself, to understand what is good and what is evil, that He help me and *inspire me* to do at all costs His holy will, without seeking anything else.

Saint Faustina Kowalska
(1905–1938)

Hers is the last humble and enamored face we wish to contemplate. She lived modestly, overlooked and contradicted until the last days of her life. But her message has echoed everywhere because of the impetus with which Saint John Paul II communicated it to the whole Church.

At the age of fifteen, after she had been rejected by various religious institutes because she had no dowry and no education, she was accepted by the Sisters of Our Lady of Mercy as a domestic worker.

For thirteen years, she was cook, gardener, caretaker at the convents of Kraków and Vilnius, rich only in her immense love for Christ.

The one who drew her out of her concealment—because He was moved by so much love—was Jesus Himself, who appeared to her one day: "He had a white robe; He was raising one hand in blessing and with the other was opening the fold of His robe over His chest, from which two large rays were emanating, one red and the other white." And He told her that He wanted to be depicted this way in an image to be spread throughout the world, accompanied by the words *Jesus, I trust in you.*

From that day on, Faustina was flooded with revelations and messages on the infinite Mercy of God and on the devotion this had to be given in the Church.

Jesus often called her and treated her like "a secretary" who was to transcribe and communicate everything. There was evidently no lack of fellow Sisters and acquaintances who, instead, called her "eccentric, hysterical, and delusional".

So when Faustina became gravely ill at the age of thirty-three, even her illnesses were not taken very seriously. And there were those who made her feel the weight of her evident "uselessness". But this was how Faustina was able to experience, in her own flesh, the encounter between the misery of creatures and the tenderness of the Creator, becoming herself "all mercy".

The most beautiful memory that remains of her—and that goes back to before she had any revelations—is the testimony of a young fellow Sister who describes her like this: "Whatever she did, we had the impression that she was doing it for someone special. She loved the Lord Jesus so tenderly, the way spouses, or better, the engaged, love each other in this world. I don't know how to express it. . . . She thought only of Him."

The way the engaged love each other: this is precisely the ecclesial mission of the *enamored* saints, called to experience and unveil the divine secret hidden in every other form of love.

CHAPTER III

Dying of Ecclesial Passion

In the previous chapter, we contemplated ten faces of saints enamored of Christ, to the point of *dying of love for Him*. Only Saint Rita of Cascia and Saint Josephine Bakhita had to wait until old age (while manifesting a certain spiritual "impatience") in order finally to meet their Bridegroom. The others reached at most the same age as Jesus.

Not that dying at a young age is decisive for holiness, but it may suggest to us the thought that, at times, Christ may also display the amorous impatience of the Bridegroom.

Now we will contemplate ten more faces of saints who had a love for Jesus that was just as intense but who died, so to speak, *of ecclesial passion*: they had, in fact, the mission—in the second millennium of Christian history—of "personifying" the Church-as-Bride, living and dying by her dramas and for her needs.

It can be said of them that they were all like the wise woman of whom Sacred Scripture speaks: the one who "builds the house" of the Bridegroom (Prov 14:1), while "the heart of [Him] trusts in her" (Prov 31:11).

Saint Clare of Assisi
(1194–1253)

She is the first we would like to recall, and it is beautiful to contemplate her right away already dying on her cot but still waiting, as happens to certain mothers who are not able to leave before they have completed their whole mission.

She too, in fact, had a last desire in her heart that would not leave her in peace: at the end of her long experience, she had finally written the rule for her Sisters (the first rule composed by a woman!), and she wanted the pope to confirm definitively, with his seal, that *privilege of poverty* ("Not to want anything, if not Our Lord") which Francis had desired so much.

For more than twenty-five years, the saint of Assisi had been in heaven (canonized just two years after his death!) and Clare had continued his work in the women's branch of the order. Now all she needed was to be able to kiss that *pontifical seal* and the next day to die.

And Pope Innocent IV came. He was coming back from the Council of Lyon and had been away from Italy for years. He was deeply moved as he stepped inside the poor little cell.

"Holy Father," Clare said, "I need to be forgiven for all my sins."

"My daughter," the pope answered, "would to heaven my need for forgiveness were like yours!"

Then she made her request, which the pontiff granted willingly. When on the next day a cardinal arrived to deliver the longed-for pontifical bull, Clare kissed it as she had desired. The next day she died.

During her last moments, they had heard her murmur, "Go with confidence, because you have a good escort. Go

with confidence, because He who created you has sancti-
fied you and, protecting you always as a mother protects
her child, has loved you with tender love."

They asked her to whom she was addressing those words.
She answered, "I am speaking to my blessed soul."

And she added, "May You be blessed, O Lord, who created me!"

Saint Bridget of Sweden
(1303–1373)

Although she was a Swedish princess, after her husband died
in 1349 she moved with her daughters to Rome, a city the
popes had abandoned for more than forty years, voluntarily
exiled in Avignon.

Rich in special gifts and singled out by the many "revelations" the Lord granted to her, Bridget had become for the
Romans and for the faraway pontiff himself a true spiritual
guide.

She got the pope to proclaim 1350 as a jubilee year. She
herself went as a pilgrim to many shrines in Italy and pushed
herself all the way to Jerusalem to illustrate the need to return always to the roots of the Christian faith. Here she
relived the Passion of Christ in a mystical way, almost embodying the Church, the sorrowful Bride at the foot of the
Cross.

Many of her contemporaries said Bridget "was a light kin-
dled by Christ to illuminate those wicked times in which
they found themselves living."

Until the last days of her life, she continued to plead with
the pontiff to come back to Rome. Twenty years had gone
by since the jubilee, and the pope had not yet decided.

Having grown very old—she was seventy by now—

Bridget kept to her room, where they celebrated Holy Mass every morning. All the outward hardships she had lived through now flared up again inside her soul, but Our Lady calmed her distress, saying to her, "whatever temptation may come to you, pay it no heed; do not leave off praying." This kept her serene, and those who visited her during her last days said "she was sweet and smiling with everyone."

The last words Bridget spoke—she who had to go through so much effort to speak and to write—were to her daughter Karin, almost as if to point out for her the simple path of holiness: "Patience and silence!"

Her confessor and confidant recounts: "Five days before Bridget died, Our Lord Jesus Christ came, stood before the altar that had been set up in her room, and said to her, 'I have done with you what the Bridegroom does when He hides from the Bride in order to make her desire Him more ardently.'"

In this desire to meet Him, finally satisfied, Bridget died.

Saint Catherine of Siena
(1347–1380)

Bridget, then, had closed her eyes without having succeeded in convincing the pope to leave Avignon. But the same tireless passion to bring him back to Rome had been inherited by the very young Catherine of Siena.

When Gregory XI finally decided to return to the Holy City (in 1376, but he made it back only in time to die there), Catherine was only thirty years old, but she was already destroyed by the apostolic exertions she had borne.

What crushed her for good was a new and unexpected wound for the Church: after the election of the new pope, in fact, some of the cardinals had rebelled, producing a great schism that would drag on for about forty years.

By this time, Catherine could only pray. Although she could hardly walk anymore, she had made a vow to go every morning to Saint Peter's, to "keep the Bridegroom company, since He has been abandoned, too", although she was so exhausted they had to support her as she made her way along the street.

This last laborious daily pilgrimage of hers had become a symbol: it was the only means she still had to help Pope Urban VI in his fight against division.

When she reached the basilica, which represents the heart of Christendom, Catherine always stopped in front of the mosaic painted by Giotto (at the time, it was in the middle of the pediment atop the colonnade) that depicted the Gospel scene of the little boat tossed by the waves in the storm, a symbol of the Church that seems to be going adrift but that nothing can sink.

This is how she herself described it:

When it is the hour of terce, I rise from Mass, and you would see a dead woman go to Saint Peter's. I enter anew to labour in the ship of the Holy Church. There I stay thus till near the hour of vespers; and from this place I would depart neither day nor night until I see this people at least a little steadily established in peace with their father. This body of mine remains without any food, without even a drop of water: in such sweet physical tortures as I never at any time endured; insomuch that my life hangs by a thread. Now I do not know what the Divine Goodness will do with me: as my feelings go, I do not say that I perceive His will in this matter; but as to my physical sensations, it seems to me that this time I am to confirm them with a new martyrdom in the sweetness of my

soul—that is, for Holy Church; then, perhaps, He will
make me rise again with Him. He will put so an end to
my miseries and to my crucified desires. . . . I have prayed
and pray His mercy that His will be fulfilled in me (Letter
373).[1]

She was not able, however, to complete her vow: on the
third Sunday of Lent, she collapsed in front of the mosaic
while she was praying there; it seemed to her—she said—
that all the weight of that little boat had been loaded onto
her frail shoulders.

They took her back to her little cell on Via del Papa (even
the details have a tenderness of their own), and she remained
unmoving there for about eight weeks, in a protracted death
agony. On the Sunday before the Ascension, everyone had
the impression she was still waging an unspeakable battle.
She said, "The only cause of my death is my ardent love
for the Church, which is consuming me."

She expired at three in the afternoon, at the age of thirty-
three, invoking the blood of Jesus and repeating his words,
"Father, into your hands I commend my spirit."

At the end of the second millennium, both Bridget of
Sweden and Catherine of Siena were proclaimed Patronesses
of Europe.

Saint Angela Merici
(1474–1540)

She lived in an era that was difficult for women. Although
historians today may speak of humanism and Renaissance,
women at the time found themselves driven backward with

[1] *Saint Catherine of Siena as Seen in Her Letters*, trans. and ed. Vida D. Scud-
der (London: Dent; New York: Dutton, 1905), pp. 349–50.

respect to the positions they had reached before. The young women of the common people, without education or dowry, often were unable to get married or be accepted into a convent, and their fate was often that of being reduced to situations of degradation and corruption, ultimately ending up in the sanatorium or the poorhouse.

And even those who "went into service" in the homes of the noble and of the rich rarely escaped forced corruption.

Of course, the Church was permeated with a powerful movement of reform, but no one seemed capable of facing such a drama, even if in Brescia there was one woman who felt the urgency of this in her heart.

Back when she was a child, Angela Merici had seen a vision of a marvelous procession of girls coming down from heaven, but at the age of sixty, she had not yet found a way to make her dream of a better life for women come true.

She went as a pilgrim to the Holy Land, but by the time she got there, she had been left blind by a sudden and mysterious disease. She took advantage of this to visit the holy places entirely absorbed within her interior world.

When she returned, she finally felt ready, in part because by this time "Jesus was crying aloud in her heart" that it was time to act. So she created a new form of religious life, calling around herself women who wanted to consecrate themselves to God but without retiring to a convent. In her *Society*, Angela gathered together both noble and prosperous women who were committed to acting as mothers and guides for girls with no social resources as well as those young women who cheerfully accepted the condition of virginity while still remaining in the world.

In practice, Angela Merici's holy brilliance drove her to elicit within her city an "impetus of social motherhood", a movement of charity of which she herself was mother. The structure devised was so flexible that Merici's institute could adapt itself to different times and places, and her *Ursulines* (a name taken from the medieval legend of Saint Ursula and her "eleven thousand virgin companions") became the top pick in the field of girls' education.

When Angela died in Brescia, several witnesses said a star had shone for three days straight over the church where her body had been laid, almost as if to recall that she had illuminated the whole city, driving it to take on a "more maternal" structure.

Saint Teresa of Ávila
(1515–1582)

Born in Ávila, in a century full of ecclesial convulsions, she became a nun at the age of twenty but converted definitively only when she understood she had to focus her entire self upon Christ alone, true God and true man, in order to be able to embrace at the same time all the divine and all the human. In this way, she embodied the image of the Church, the enamored and diligent bride, who tirelessly builds many dwellings for Jesus-as-Eucharist. It was for this end that she reformed the Carmelite Order, founding seventeen monasteries in Spain, where she gathered souls desirous of living "for God alone and in His company". To them she left the exemplary account of her own life, which had become "prayer", and the invitation to "walk toward perfection" with joy, to the point of experiencing that mystical marriage which is the true destiny of souls. Also characteristic of Teresa was the apostolic and ecclesial purpose she attributed to the contemplative experience, in the persuasion that God never intends to coddle souls but always to *give them to the world*, as He did with His own Son, Jesus.

At the end of her life—saddened by the thought of thousands of souls unaware of their own dignity and slaves of themselves—she wrote *The Interior Castle* (a symbol of every soul), explaining how to enter it and how to proceed through the *Mansions*, finally penetrating the most intimate room where it is possible for everyone to receive from Christ that unitive kiss invoked by the Bride of the *Song of Songs* (cf. Song 1:2, 7:9, 8:1).

In 1582, in the monastery of Alba de Tormes, Teresa lived her death as a daughter of the Church, certain everything was finally about to be fulfilled:

> At five in the evening, she asked for the Most Holy Sacrament, and by this time she was so poorly that she was no longer able to move in her bed. . . . When she realized that they were coming with the Eucharist and saw entering through the door of the cell that Lord whom she loved so much—even though she was so prostrate and weighed down beneath a deadly languor that kept her from so much as turning herself—she sat up without anyone's help, almost as if she were trying to cast herself out of the bed and needed to be held back. . . . She said: "O my Lord and my Bridegroom, the hour has come that I have so greatly desired. It is now time for us to be united, it is time for me to come to you."[2] Around nine in the evening—shortly before she died—her face lit up in a remarkable way, it became radiant, and the hand holding the crucifix closed with such strength that they were no longer able to take it away from her. She died moving her lips and smiling as if she were speaking with Someone who had finally arrived.

The nuns of all the monasteries afterward recounted the miracles that were happening all over while their mother was

---

[2] The first biographer changed these words of Teresa for the sake of modesty, having her exclaim: "It is time for us to see each other!" But the testimonies of the nuns present at her passing are almost unanimous.

dying. Those of Alba de Tormes recounted the most delicate miracle: in front of the window of the cell in which
Teresa was dying there was a little dried-up tree that had
stopped bearing flowers or fruit. And it happened that after
that night, in the morning, the little tree was completely
covered with flowers white as snow.

And this because, if Teresa had loved Jesus like a Bridegroom, Jesus had loved Teresa even more.

Saint Elizabeth Ann Seton
(1774–1821)

She was born in New York, to a Protestant family. At the
age of twenty, she married the eldest son of one of the most
illustrious and wealthy New York families, which had business ties in Italy. Her husband, who was very sickly, died
during a trip to Tuscany, leaving her alone with five children. Elizabeth Ann had to stay for several months as the
guest of friends in Livorno, which gave her the chance to
see the true Catholic faith up close, and she felt a strong
attraction for the Eucharist. She felt she had always desired
it without knowing she did so and that she had always suffered from its absence. So after she returned to the United
States, she decided to become Catholic, although this cost
her the rejection of her rich relatives.

In order to survive financially, she decided to educate her
five children herself while also taking on other students. In
1808, she met a French missionary who invited her to Bal-
timore (the center of Catholicism in the United States at
the time) to open a small religious school for girls. Elizabeth thus founded the institute of the Sisters of Charity, the
first women religious of America and the beginning of the

whole parish school system employed in the United States down to our own day. In this way, she dedicated herself to educating both her own children and all those entrusted to her by Catholic families in the city.

She nonetheless experienced the drama of the mother who is able to educate the children of others but can get nothing out [some] of her own. Even on her deathbed, she prayed for the salvation of their souls, asking God to take care of her reckless youngsters, while she became—for all the other children heaven entrusted to her—"sweet Providence".

Her last illness drew from her lips nothing but acts of abandonment to God, "Our God is our all. God alone is all."

And if she asked for anything, she asked for the Eucharist, "Only give Him to me!"

To the sisters gathered around her deathbed she said, echoing the famous last invocation of Saint Teresa of Ávila: "Be children of the Church! Be children of the Church!"

When she died, she had experienced all the female vocations (as wife, mother, widow, consecrated woman, educator) and is therefore venerated as mother and protector of the Catholic Church in the United States.

Blessed Victoire Rasoamanarivo
(1848–1894)

She was born in Antananarivo, in 1848, to a noble Madagascar family. She converted to Christianity at the age of sixteen, when she was able to meet the first French missionaries and sisters who attended to her education. She married her cousin Ratsimatahodriaka and was always faithful to him, even though she had to suffer on account of his unworthy and vicious behavior. In 1868, there rose to the throne a queen who, for political reasons, decided to adhere definitively to Christianity but selected Protestantism as the state religion. Countless forms of pressure were then brought to bear on Victoire to convince her to apostatize: threats of being relegated among the slaves or being deprived of social rights. Little by little, she succeeded in gaining everyone's respect, so evident were her goodness, boundless charity (in particular for the slaves, whom she treated as if they were her children), unalterable dignity.

In 1883, following a further conflict with France, all the Catholic missionaries (who were of French origin) were expelled from the island, and around 80,000 Catholics were left on their own. So, before they left, the missionaries asked the Madagascar princess to be herself "the guardian angel of the Catholic mission and the support of the Christians". According to testimonies from the time, "Victoire became the foundation, the pillar, the father and mother of all the Christians, as the holy Virgin was after Jesus left for heaven."

Her wisdom, her prestige, and her energy prevented divisions among the Catholics; her charity toward the poor, lepers, prisoners, and slaves kept the community's heart beating; her generosity made possible even the financial survival of the Catholic community, made up of humble and poor people.

Finally, in 1886, the missionaries were able to return, and Victoire humbly restored the community into their hands, continuing to offer to all her exemplary life of charity.

In recompense, God granted her to receive into her arms and baptize at the point of death her husband, who had been the victim of an indecorous incident and had finally repented.

Left a widow, she spent the last six years of her life in an ever more intense maternal outpouring of prayer and an ever more expansive charity.

She died at the age of forty-six, lifting up her hands, in which, as usual, she was holding the rosary, and saying aloud three times, "Mother, mother, mother!"

Perhaps she was invoking Our Lady, as she was accustomed to do. Perhaps in that cry were united all the dramas of her life: the desire for those children she had never had in her poor and difficult marriage, the ecclesial task that had been asked of her and that she had carried out with every fiber of her being . . .

But that last word certainly described her perfectly in the vocation and mission God had entrusted to her regarding His people, still so young in the faith.

She has been given a title unusual in Christian history, but splendid: Mother of the Church of Madagascar.

Saint Frances Xavier Cabrini
(1850–1917)

During the years in which she worked, there were about fourteen million Italian immigrants on the American continent: at that time, they were an anonymous people, "white slaves", crowded into human hutches, forced to live in physically and often also morally brutalizing conditions. They lived without schools, without hospitals, without churches, quite often without jobs.

Frances arrived in New York, with seven companions, at the end of March 1889. On account of their initiative, generosity, and charity, right away the Italian sisters won the esteem not only of their countrymen but also of the native-born. They worked above all for the integration of the new generations, creating a dense network of schools, boarding houses, orphanages, nursing homes. In thirty-seven years of activity, Mother Cabrini set up around sixty-seven educational and hospital institutes, crossing the Atlantic dozens of times and repeatedly traversing the two Americas from one cape to the other. She said travel had become as natural to her as walking down "the garden path". And she added, "The world is too small! I would like to embrace the whole of it!"

To her missionary sisters, she always repeated, "Jesus is for us a blessed necessity."

In her youthful diary, she had written: "O adorable heart of Jesus, what fate do you have in store for me? I desire to die of love after a life of total dedication. Give me a heart big like the universe. . . . If I had the means I would build a ship and call it *Cristoforo*, after him who carried Christ, and I would sail the whole world making Christ known to all the nations."

She died knowing her prayer had been granted.

Saint Katharine Mary Drexel
(1858–1955)

She was born in Philadelphia to a family of bankers. She learned from her mother, a profoundly Catholic and socially engaged woman, to be attentive toward the poor and the marginalized. She loved to travel but was taken aback by the misery of the people of color in the southern states and by the marginalization of Native Americans in the north. During a pilgrimage to Rome, she asked Pope Leo XIII to send missionaries to those lands, but she received this reply that set her heart on fire, "Why don't you become a missionary yourself?"

She accepted the challenge, founding the Sisters of the Blessed Sacrament "for the human promotion of Native Americans and Blacks in America", indicating the Eucharist as the source of charity for the poor and the oppressed. She was called "the richest nun in the world", but she spent everything she had on the construction of 145 missions and around sixty schools where there were no longer "children of slaves" and "children of savages" but only "children of God" who had the right to be loved, educated, and brought up like the children of the whites. She even founded the first university institute (Xavier University) open to Native Americans and Blacks.

The difficulties and persecutions Katharine had to undergo were innumerable because of social prejudices that were so deeply rooted they had even influenced the Church. At the time, it was difficult to find white priests willing to provide religious assistance for those marginalized people. And in the religious institutes, the vocations of persons of color were not looked upon favorably.

Today, many wonder "what the Catholic Church might have been like in respect to minorities had she not come along. She saved the Church from embarrassment in terms of social justice."[3]

Mother Katharine died at the age of almost one hundred, happy she had finally been able to see the repeal (during the very last years of her life and, in part, thanks to her) of laws of racial segregation.

She had spent her last seventeen years almost immobilized

---

[3] Paschal Baumann, quoted at franciscanmedia.org/franciscan-spirit-blog/the-legacy-of-saint-katharine-drexel.

in body, but certainly not in spirit, completely focused on adoring the Eucharist, the first love of her life.

She died with this tender prayer on her lips: "O Divine Spirit, I wish to be before you as a light feather, so that your breath may carry me where you will."

Saint Edith Stein
(1891–1942)

She died as a victim of the Nazi persecution, so we could have placed her story among those of the martyrs. But we prefer to privilege her "motherly face", since Saint John Paul II selected her as Patroness of Europe together with Saint Catherine of Siena and Saint Bridget of Sweden.

Born to a Jewish family in Breslau in 1891, she grew up proud of her German nationality and culture but less tied to her religious origins. She attended the universities of Göttingen and Freiburg—something rare at the time for a woman—and did not hesitate to identify herself as an atheist, even though she carefully emphasized that the search for truth was her prayer. She was a student and admirer of Edmund Husserl and his branch of phenomenology. Taught to pay close attention "to phenomena", maintaining and defending the purity of thought and the objectivity of experience, she discovered with admiration the Christian faith of some of her colleagues. She converted to Catholicism after she read the *Life* of Saint Teresa of Ávila and realized, "Here is the truth!", and this also allowed her to recover the most authentic roots of Judaism. Baptized in 1922, she taught pedagogy for a decade and dedicated herself to the composition of philosophical works of notable value. In 1934, she entered the Carmelite monastery of Cologne, where she took the name of Teresa Benedicta of the Cross.

On account of the racial persecution unleashed by Hitler, she was transferred to the monastery in Echt, in Holland, but she was arrested by the Nazis all the same in retaliation against the Catholic bishops of the country.

Edith was, therefore, Jew, philosopher, teacher, writer, convert, Carmelite, martyr, personifying the most diverse expressions of central European female identity and completely realizing, in the end, that "dignity of woman" which she had always taught and defended with passion.

Surprisingly familiar (and maternal) is also the last image of Edith Stein, as it has been described for us by a Jewish merchant from Cologne, who met her in the concentration and transit camp of Westerbork (before she was transferred to Auschwitz, where she was killed):

> Among the prisoners who were brought in on 5 August, Sr. Benedicta stood out on account of her great calmness and composure. The distress in the barracks, and the stir caused by the new arrivals, was indescribable. Sr. Benedicta was just like an angel, going around among the women, comforting them, helping them and calming them. Many of the mothers were near to distraction; they had not bothered about their children the whole day long, but just sat brooding in dumb despair. Sr. Benedicta took care of the little children, washed them and combed them, looked after their feeding and their other needs. During the whole of her stay there, she was so busy washing and cleaning as acts of lovingkindness that everyone was astonished.[4]

In a letter from a few years before, when she was already preparing to give her life for her people, Edith had written: "I am confident that the Lord has accepted my life for everyone. I am reminded repeatedly of Queen Esther who

[4] An account given by Julius Markan, quoted by Teresia Renata Posselt, O.C.D., in: *Edith Stein: The Life of a Philosopher and Carmelite* (Washington, D.C.: ICS Publications, 2005), p. 217.

was taken from her people precisely to stand before the king for the people. I am a very poor and powerless Esther, but the King who has chosen me is eternally great and compassionate."[5]

She died in the gas chamber in Auschwitz on August 9, 1942.

~

In conclusion, we can say all these saints lived and died of ecclesial passion, because they were so closely tied to the Bridegroom Christ that they wanted to be identified with the Church-as-Bride, participating in all her needs and all her dramas.

All of them, in fact, although in different and personalized ways, heard with passion, joy, and obedience the invitation Christ issued one day to Saint Teresa of Ávila: "From now on not only will you look after My honor as being the honor of your Creator, King, and God, but you will look after it as My true bride. My honor is yours, and yours Mine."[6]

---

[5] Quoted by Father Paul Hamans in *Edith Stein and Companions on the Way to Auschwitz*, trans. Sister M. Regina van den Berg, F.S.G.M. (San Francisco: Ignatius Press, 2010), p. 74.

[6] Teresa of Ávila, *Spiritual Testimony* no. 31, in the *Collected Works of St. Teresa of Ávila*, vol. 1, trans. Kieran Kavanaugh, O.C.D., and Otilio Rodriguez, O.C.D. (Washington, D.C.: ICS Publications; Institute of Carmelite Studies, 1976), p. 336.

CHAPTER IV

Dying of Maternal Charity

The distinctions we are suggesting in the following chapters have a purely pedagogical value: in fact, all the saints display the spousal love with which they ended their lives, the ecclesial passion that consumed them, and the fervor with which they practiced this or that work of mercy, consuming themselves with charity.

In this chapter, however, we will seek to contemplate the merciful face of certain saints who, until their last breath, practiced charity toward the weak and marginalized.

Saint Elizabeth of Hungary
(1207–1231)

Her contemporaries called her "an extraordinary wonder of our time".

In fact, her story has all the enchantment of "the marvelous fable of a queen who became the servant of the poor and sick", a fable that in this case, however, is history.

She had a hospital built near her castle of Wartburg in Thuringia, gathering sick and poor people of all kinds there. And it was said that during the first years of their marriage, her husband, who greatly loved and supported her, got upset with her only one time: when he was told that, as Elizabeth could find nowhere else to put a dying leper, she had laid him down on their marriage bed. But it was also recounted that when the covers were taken from the bed, he had seen imprinted upon it the image of the Crucified.

The difficulties came after her husband died, when her relatives disinherited her. She then moved to Marburg, where her confessor lived, founding a hospital there and dedicating herself personally to the everyday care of the sick.

Here we contemplate her during the last months of her young life, when she was "completely worn out by compassion", as her confessor describes her:

> Before her death I heard her confession and asked her what should be done with her possessions. She answered that what seemed to belong to her was all for the poor and begged me to distribute everything to them, with the exception of a tunic of no value that she was wearing and in which she wanted to be buried. After this she received the Body of the Lord. Then, until the evening, she thought back on all the beautiful things she had heard in preaching.

She dwelt in particular on the Gospel episode of the raising of Lazarus, especially on how Jesus wept before the tomb of his friend, and the memory seemed to enchant her.

Then it grew dark. Toward midnight they heard her exclaim, "This is the hour in which the Virgin brought forth her Child!"

And she expired "as if sweetly falling asleep". She was only twenty-four and had spent almost every one of those years defending the sublime Christian dignity of all the poor of her kingdom.

The historians say Elizabeth "is one of the sweetest, warmest, most agreeable saints of the whole Middle Ages". And a modern theologian has proposed for her the title of "Saint of Social Justice".

The portrait of Elizabeth of Hungary is so intense it could summarize the feminine history of charity during the first fifteen centuries of the Christian era. And it allows us to dive right into the second half of the second millennium, when the possibility was opening up within the Church, for consecrated women as well, to unite the contemplative and active life in order to respond to the most urgent ecclesial necessities in the fields of education, charity, mission.

This meant the ideal of "virgins enamored of Christ" could be brought together with the ideal of "virgin mothers" who take care of God's children and could also manifest their twofold passion in the way in which they offer themselves to God at the end of their earthly existence.

And it is interesting to observe that for some of these, this twofold ideal is grafted onto a previous and arduous experience of marriage and motherhood.

Saint Catherine of Genoa
(1447–1510)

She was married at the age of sixteen to the Genoese prince Giuliano Adorno, and for ten years she joined him in his dissipated way of life. Then she converted, pulling her husband along on her "holy adventure". She became "rector" of a big hospital (something unprecedented at the time) and had to confront the most serious plague of the century. Around her a movement took shape of men and women, religious and clerics, nobles and middle class, literati and humanists, physicians and notaries, shopkeepers and populace, who helped her in charity and recognized her as a mother and spiritual guide. She thus became the inspiration for that society or fraternity that was later called the Oratory of Divine Love, which was to give rise, throughout

all of Italy, to the true Catholic Reformation, founded, not
on controversy and theological debates, but on a renewed
love for the mystery of the Incarnation and on missionary
dedication to the needs of the Church.

The sick in the hospitals, the beggars and the destitute,
the plague-ridden and the incurable, the orphans and the
foundlings, the lost women and the "at-risk" girls, the imprisoned and the convicts, those condemned to death, the
abandoned elderly, the insane, the slaves, the dying were
thus not only assisted but honored like Christ Himself (and
it was in this above all that contemplative falling in love consisted).

In the last nine years of her life, Catherine was prey to a
strange malady that the doctors were not able to diagnose,
but she would say with a smile, "Mine is not a malady that
is in need of medicine."

And when she spoke of her *true* malady—Love—those
who heard her wept. They said that "in listening to her
words, they saw heaven, and in looking at her martyred
body, they saw purgatory." In fact, in accord with the mission God had given her, Catherine of Genoa had a very long
death agony in which unspeakable torments on account of
her separation from God alternated with moments of heavenly joy over His imminent manifestation. In essence, she
seemed like the embodiment of that "doctrine of purgatory"
which she had explained so well in her celebrated treatise.

She said about her horrendous sufferings, "May every
passion and every torment be welcome in me, if this is
God's sweet plan." Certain other days, however, she lived
"in a nimbus of gladness and smiles", like an anticipation
of heaven. And she spoke of death—which would resolve
that devastating drama—as "sweet, gracious, and kindly".

She died in a little white cell in the hospital, and her followers who surrounded her bore witness: "With great peace

and tranquility, she gently expired from this life and went to her sweet Love."

Saint Jane Frances de Chantal
(1572–1641)

She was a wife and mother. Widowed at the age of twenty-nine, she entrusted herself to the spiritual guidance of Saint Francis de Sales, who helped her to experience "how human is the divine and how divine is the human." They decided together to found a new women's institute focused on works of mercy. They called it the Visitation, in memory of the charity with which the holy Virgin had run off to visit and assist her cousin Elizabeth, who had become pregnant at an advanced age. They were not able, however, to give it the apostolic and charitable openness they wanted, because the ecclesiastical laws at the time required that women be clois-tered. But they were able to give it a character of humanity and tenderness, allowing the frail to become sisters, and even the sick and elderly. And the initiative spread like wildfire, requiring Jane to found during her lifetime no fewer than eighty-seven monasteries.

This took her all over France, and everywhere she was awaited and invoked as a saint. Even Charles IV, Duke of Lorraine, publicly called her "the saint of our century".

On the night of December 12, 1641, the last of her life, feeling death was near, she asked to have the account of Saint Monica's death in Ostia read to her. Then, listening to the prayers for the dying, she sighed, "How beautiful they are!"

But the agony was prolonged, and she suffered unspeak-ably for days. At last she grew quiet. The priest attending to her reminded her of the parable of the ten virgins waiting for the arrival of the Bridegroom, in order to welcome Him with lamps alight, and she said rapturously, "Yes, my Father, I am going. Jesus, Jesus, Jesus!"

Saint Louise de Marillac
(1591–1660)

She, too, had been wife and mother, but she bore count-less emotional scars on account of the many disgraces she had undergone in her family. She found redemption with the spiritual help of Saint Francis de Sales, who put her in touch with Saint Vincent de Paul. Although Louise and Vin-cent were very far apart in terms of social background and mentality, they discovered they had the same heart when it came to Jesus and His poor. And this brought them together in the same charity, to the point that Vincent was seized with admiration and great tenderness for this spiritual daughter of his who had become such a mature and wise, vibrant and sweet companion. One day he wrote to her: "God alone knows what I am for you and what you are for me. . . . My heart is no longer mine, but yours in that of Our Lord."

Already in 1547, seeing that Louise was consuming all of her physical energies in charity, Vincent said of her: "Con-sidering the natural order of things, I maintain she has been dead for ten years now; to see her one would say she is coming from the tomb, so frail is her body and so pallid her face. But God knows what power of spirit she has within her!"

In fact, Louise lived another thirteen years. On her death-bed, she asked to be able to see, for the last time, the friend and father of her soul, but Vincent—unable to go to her—sent this message: "Mademoiselle, you are departing before me. If God forgives my sins, I hope to meet you soon in heaven."

And this is what happened: they were in fact together again in heaven six months later.

Saint Catherine Labouré
(1806–1876)

She was a poor farmer's daughter who, orphaned at the age of twelve, had to take into her own hands the whole management of her large family, the farm, and the household chores. Only at the age of twenty-four did she succeed in realizing her vocation among the Daughters of Charity of Saint Vincent de Paul.

Right away they said of her that "she was pious, had a good character and a strong temperament, loved work and was very cheerful." But the social and political situation of the time was sad and worrisome, marked by great upheavals and by persecutions. And so it was just then that the holy Virgin revealed to the humble Catherine a heaven-sent remedy: the striking of a Miraculous Medal (which the sister contemplated in a vision, as shown to her in detail).

In spite of opposition, this was brought about, with the backing of the archbishop of Paris. The medal was fashioned by a goldsmith, and so many healings and graces of conversion were obtained through it that in a very few years millions of copies had to be struck. The newspaper *La France* was already maintaining in 1835 that the sacred little object had become "one of the greatest signs of faith in recent times".

Catherine, however, remained unknown to everyone, and only her superiors ever found out about her visions. She was known only as the sister who looked after the little orphan girls being brought up at the convent or worked at the hospice for the elderly in Enghien that had been entrusted to her community. Here she worked for forty-five years, performing the humblest offices with a smile always on her lips.

During the Franco-Prussian War of 1870, the convent was flooded with the destitute, and she was given the task of preparing more than 1,200 meals a day.

And yet, during the last years of her life, when Catherine became ill, she found herself entrusted to a nurse who was not very attentive or charitable, sometimes leaving her without food or fire, but she never complained. She would only say, "I am going away, to heaven!"

"Aren't you afraid of dying?" a very young sister asked her.

And Catherine, thinking back in her heart on the visions given to her in her youth, replied with the smile of one who knows, "Why be afraid of going to see Our Lord, His Mother, and Saint Vincent?"

For a whole lifetime, she had been waiting to *see them*! She died on the last afternoon of the year, "with sweetness and serenity", unhappy only that the little orphan girls were on vacation and could not recite around her bed the beautiful litany of the Immaculate.

Saint Maria Crocifissa di Rosa
(1813–1855)

In 1836, the city of Brescia was devastated by a cholera epidemic so violent that in a few months it had left more than thirty-two thousand dead. At the time, Paola di Rosa was just a young woman from a good family who had consecrated herself to God in her heart but was living in the world, managing her father's silk factory. Shaken by the emergency, the young industrialist convinced some of her friends and workers to volunteer at the quarantine hospital, shutting themselves up, out of love for Jesus and the poor infirm, in that frightening enclosure.

The city was moved with admiration for the courage of those young women. So when the epidemic was over, Paola found herself leading a close-knit group of thirty-two young women, and all of them agreed to offer themselves as nursing staff to take over the entire management of hospital services (in shambles at the time) in accord with the medical and administrative personnel. So she structured hospital assistance as a family business in which the different tasks did not hinder the unity of all and their equal consecration to Christ the Lord. At first a pious association of laywomen, this went on to become the Institute of the Handmaids of Charity, which little by little would take over all the hospitals in the region. Afterward, they would also care for abandoned children, deaf-mutes in particular, and soldiers wounded on the battlefield. Just three years before she died, Paola became a full-fledged religious sister, taking the name Mary Crucified of Jesus Abandoned, a name that emphasized the entirely unique interior drama she had always lived.

Ever since she had been a young woman, in fact, God had asked her to share continually in the abandonment Jesus experienced on the Cross. But it was from this difficult interior grace that she learned to contemplate Jesus in the sick and to acquire the genius of always knowing how to comfort them.

When the moment finally came for her definitive meeting with Him who had asked her for such great love as to have her relive the mystery of His holy Passion, when she was about to die, she was told that a Mass was being celebrated for her at the Shrine of Our Lady of Graces. She recollected herself in prayer. And when the Mass was finished, her face became shining, as if a pledge of resurrection and of complete peace. Smiling, she said only: "The grace is done!"

And she expired. That daughter, whom God had "abandoned" so she could share in the agonizing Passion of His Son, now found herself again entirely in the trustworthy hands of the heavenly Father.

Saint Bartolomea Capitanio
(1807–1833)

and

Saint Vincenza Gerosa
(1784–1847)

In Lovere in the province of Bergamo, which at the time was under Austrian rule, these two had decided to found the institute of the Sisters of Charity of Lovere, in order to dedicate themselves "to all the works of mercy" and, in particular, to the education of poor and abandoned young women.

The push for the foundation had come from Bartolomea (an ardent young teacher), while Vincenza (more mature and prosperous) simply wanted to help her financially in the mission she had undertaken.

But when they drew up the institute's founding documents, the former was already dying and the latter considered herself absolutely unfit to lead it. And yet from their strong and holy friendship the initiative received powerful and lasting roots.

When the foundation had just been inaugurated, Bartolomea fell gravely ill, and her little room was invaded by the noises from the construction of the nearby chapel, which she had so greatly desired. To allow her to die in peace, someone asked the stonemasons to suspend their work. But the sick woman sighed: "Let me hear those noises. They bring me joy at the thought that Jesus Eucharist will dwell in our home."

And she died with the serenity of hearing in the depths of her soul the voice of Jesus, who was saying to her: "Fear not, I am holding your little convent in my own hands."

Vincenza Gerosa, much older and less sure of herself, would live for fourteen more years and would find in God the strength she needed to found twenty-five communities (all with some initiative of education or assistance) and to act as mother to more than 170 sisters. At her death, she felt distressed at the thought that she was looked after too well and said to her daughters, almost apologizing: "Jesus Christ is on the cross, and here I am comfortable, in a bed! Lord, forgive my too great delicacy!"

On June 29, 1847, she had just received the Eucharist when they heard her repeat as if she were suddenly in a hurry: "Let me go; let me go!"

"But where?" they asked her.

"To heaven, to heaven!" she replied.

And she expired holding on tight to the crucifix in her hands.

Blessed Enrichetta Alfieri
(1891–1951)

At the age of twenty, she consecrated herself to God among the Sisters of Charity of Saint Jeanne-Antide Thouret, and after a serious illness from which she was miraculously healed, she was sent to attend to the inmates of the San

Vittore prison in Milan. Constrained by inhuman regulations, she acted with freedom and Christian imagination: into the sad and gloomy halls of the prison, through the bars of hundreds of cells, into the most horrible cellars, and within the most blinded consciences, her heart was able to peer inside and bring at least a scintilla of goodness.

She became the "angel" and the "mama" of all the inmates, above all when the Nazis turned the prison into a concentration camp for Jews and political prisoners.

Sr. Enrichetta did not limit herself to comforting and protecting them in every way possible; she also organized a true network of protection and connection for them that extended outside the prison, thwarting searches, arrests, and threats of deportation. In this way, she brought about "that *rebellion for the sake of love* which redeemed man from falsehood, cowardice, and fear" (Carlo Maria Cardinal Martini).

Every day she herself was in danger of being investigated and sentenced to death. And this is what happened when a message of warning meant to save a family of Jews ended up in the hands of the German soldiers. She was imprisoned under harsh conditions and sentenced to be deported to Germany; in the end, under pressure, they contented themselves with "confining" her to a convent where the sisters took care of impoverished minors.

After the liberation, she went back to her prison (which in the meantime had been emptied of its former prisoners and filled up again with the former persecutors, who had been arrested in turn) continuing to see even in the new inmates only brothers and sisters to be protected and loved.

She suffered serious complications from a fall, but she wanted to remain in her prison, where she experienced a long death agony while praying and offering her last pains for her charges. To her fellow Sisters, she said that after her death she preferred to be remembered with the *Gloria* rather than with the *Requiem*. But she also asked not to receive too many visits, because, she said: "I have to get myself together if I am going on the journey!"

And when they brought her the last sacraments, she confided: "I did not believe it was so sweet to die."

In a commentary on the beauty of her life, there was an endless line of female inmates who, two by two, filed past her body to kiss her hand, while they passed the same conviction from one to the other: "A saint has died, a saint has died!"

Saint Teresa of Calcutta
(1910–1997)

She was born in Albania, entering when very young into a religious congregation that sent her to India, where she became the headmistress of a Catholic school.

At the age of thirty-six, however, disturbed at the sight of a poor woman making her agonizing way along the street, her face gnawed away by rats and ants, she perceived "a call within the call". So she decided to leave the convent in order to consecrate herself to the service "of the poorest of the poor".

She founded the Missionaries of Charity, set up to care for the dying, abandoned children, deformed babies, lepers, teen mothers, prostitutes, prisoners, homeless, alcoholics, the severely handicapped, the mentally ill, drug addicts, AIDS patients. In essence, all the "wounded of the street" found in the homes of Mother Teresa a welcome and an open ear.

But it is significant to recall that Mother Teresa wanted

some of her sisters to remain exclusively dedicated to the contemplation of Jesus-as-Eucharist.

She always explained her work in the same way: "Everything we do—prayer, work, sacrifice—we do for Jesus. Our life does not have any other meaning, any motivation other than Him who loves us deeply. Jesus is the only meaning of our life."

She was almost seventy years old when she was awarded the Nobel Peace Prize, and she used the opportunity to defend before that prestigious academy the rights of children not yet born. She still had eighteen years of apostolic labors ahead of her. Venerated by all, she felt like nothing more than a "poor pencil" that God had wanted to use: "Very often I feel like a little pencil in God's hands. He does the writing, He does the thinking, He does the movement, I have only to be the pencil."

It seems that even during the last years of her life, God asked her—as he does with the greatest mystics—to bear the trial of interior darkness, allowing her to share in the sufferings of Christ on Calvary and even those of all non-believers.

She accepted, saying humbly: "I have come to love the darkness, for I believe now that it is a part, a very, very small part of Jesus' darkness and pain on earth."[1]

Servant of God Annalena Tonelli
(1943–2003)

Born in Forlì in 1943, at the age of twenty-six, she decided to go to Africa as a lay missionary. This is how she explained

[1] Beatified on October 19, 2003, Mother Teresa of Calcutta was subsequently recognized as a saint and canonized on September 4, 2016.—ED.

her decision: "I decided to be for others—the poor, the suffering, the abandoned, the unloved—when I was a child, and
so I have been and trust I will continue to be until the end
of my life. I wanted to follow only Jesus Christ. Nothing
else interested me so strongly: Him and the poor in Him.
For Him I made a choice of radical poverty."

For thirty-five years, she worked in Kenya and Somalia,
setting up, first, a special school for deaf-mutes and disabled
children and, then, an anti-tuberculosis center for thousands
of patients, devising new preventive measures that are now
recognized by the World Health Organization and used all
over the world.

Her only desire was that "the lowly, the voiceless, those
who count for nothing in the eyes of the world but for so
much in the eyes of God, his well-beloved, could get back
up again by holding on to her neck and supported by her
embrace."

Dearly loved by the Muslim patients of her little hospital,
she was, however, hated by those who wanted to get their
hands on the meager funding she received from Italy.

On the evening of October 5, 2003 (the day before seeing
the completion of a new wing of her little hospital), while
she was alone in the company of the Eucharist (which the
bishop brought to her periodically so she could live with
her Lord and adore him), Annalena was killed with two rifle shots in the back of her head.

Just a few days before, she had written to a priest friend,
speaking to him about Jesus-as-Eucharist just as one speaks
about a dear person with whom one lives:

"Over there is He. And since I have been at the desk, His
voice has not left me. By now I know it by memory, because I bear it written in my heart. 'Come be with me,' He
says to me, 'nothing is more important than prayer. I know.

I can do all. I, I alone!' I know His voice better than my own, better than my thoughts. He fills me with a certainty of heaven and an irrepressible eagerness to remain there, but also with that quite clear disquiet over the suffering of the world and with the sole commandment to plunge into it and to love it with desperate strength."

She knew she was risking her life, but she had long been prepared for this.

Writing to friends a few months before the tragedy, she had confided: "I would like all those I love to learn to see death with simplicity. Dying is like living. My death, my illness, my pain are not at all different from the death, the illness, the pain of these adults and children who die before our eyes day after day. My life is for them, for these little patients, for those mutilated in body and spirit, for the unfortunate who have not deserved it. If only I could live and die of love! Will it be granted to me?"

It was not until three weeks after the attack that a missionary was able to visit the village and the little hospital Annalena had taken care of, and unexpectedly he found still wrapped in a white handkerchief, inside a small container, the consecrated host, waiting in the desert of Somalia.

If only I could live and die of love!: this is the last wish of a martyr of charity, expressed in a formula that unites all four of the chapters we have written so far and already anticipates the many accounts that still lie ahead.

CHAPTER V

Dying of Paternal Charity

In the encyclical *Deus Caritas est*, Pope Benedict XVI told the Church: "The Christian's programme—the programme of the Good Samaritan, the programme of Jesus—is 'a heart which sees'. This heart sees where love is needed and acts accordingly" (no. 31b).

Although they are equally capable of tenderness and intelligence, the eyes of a mother and those of a father, nonetheless, look differently at the needs of the children: the mother's gaze is more immediate and immediately nurturing and inviting; that of the father is more bent on planning structures and organizations (sometimes even a whole city, as Cottolengo did) or intervening with the government of a nation (as Vincent de Paul did) or revolutionizing the social system (as Martin de Porres did) or being recognized as a national hero (as Damien De Veuster was).

And we can add that the holy mothers of charity die with the preoccupation *that perhaps they did not love enough*, while the holy fathers of charity die, almost always, with a little drama in their hearts: *that they did not do enough*.

But the charity is the same.

Through the experiences recounted in this chapter, therefore, we have privileged—among the many possible faces —those of certain saints who created new models of social life.

Saint Girolamo Miani (or Emiliani)
(1481–1537)

As a young man, he had chosen the career of a soldier, quickly rising through the ranks of the military hierarchy. In 1508, he was governor and defender of Castelnuovo, near Treviso, but was defeated and taken prisoner. He miraculously succeeded in escaping and decided to change his life, dedicating himself to the assistance of the poor and the sick.

The famine and plague of 1528 that accompanied the invasion of the Landsknechte left Venice in tatters, and, in assisting the sick and the dying, Girolamo used up all his resources. But it was above all the deplorable situation of the orphans that tore at his heart. He gathered some of them around him and tried to get them to learn a trade. He lived, worked, prayed with them. And he made available to them master craftsmen, benefactors, and educators.

From Venice he went to Verona, Brescia, Bergamo, Como, and finally Milan: everywhere he had been invited by the local nobility, who wanted to entrust to him the organization of assistance for the poor in their lands. But Girolamo accepted no interference and no bribes. To Francesco Sforza, who had sent him a large sum to entice him, he dispatched a messenger: "Tell the duke that I would lose too great a treasure if, having come to Milan poor, I were to leave rich." He always arrived with a little entourage of orphans who had become his friends and assistants, gradually joined by the abandoned children of the area. During harvest time, he sent them to give a hand to the poor farmers, and the boys spontaneously became teachers of catechism, of songs, and of prayers.

Although he did not accept money with strings attached, Girolamo accepted gifts of every kind for his protégés and his run-down buildings, to turn them into orphanages and workshops or into shelters for the "repentant girls" he got away from the street and from vice.

In the end, he set up his general headquarters in Somasca (a town on the border between the duchy of Milan and the Venetian republic), where he laid the foundations of the Congregation of Regular Clerics at the Service of Orphans. He, however, always remained a layman.

In 1537, the plague, erupting with new violence, struck him in Somasca while he was personally assisting his poor, sick little orphans.

Before stretching out on his cot, he wanted to wash the feet of the little orphans who were in the house, in imitation of Christ at the Last Supper. Afterward, on the white wall against which his bed stood, he drew a big red cross. He lay down and turned toward the cross in order to be able to die while contemplating it and almost as if he were taking his ease on it. It was his Good Friday, but already glorious with the Resurrection.

To his coworkers (among whom certain divisions had already sprung up that had saddened him) he humbly said: "I will be of more use to you there than here."

They watched him dying, amazed at how meek and serene he was, but he said he had "come to terms with Christ".

And it seemed to them—as they later testified—"that he had heaven in his grasp".

Saint John of God
(1495–1550)

João Cidade Duarte, of Portuguese origin, had been a shepherd, a farmer, a soldier, a peddler, a bookseller, but without ever finding the right vocation. Then he had converted, with such passion and verve they had thought he was crazy and put him in an asylum.

The asylum was a decisive experience for him: seeing up close the inhumanity of the treatment methods in vogue at the time, he devoted himself to the other patients with such dedication and intelligence as to obtain his own release. He became known as John of God.

So he decided, at the age of forty-four, to give himself voluntarily to the care of the infirm (the mentally ill, above all), housing a few of them in a cottage. In the evening, he went around the neighborhoods on higher ground with a basket on his back for collecting alms, crying aloud: "Who wants to do some good for himself? My brothers, for the love of God, do some good for yourselves."

And *Fatebenefratelli* ended up becoming his motto and even the nickname of the Brothers Hospitallers, the religious order he inspired.

In time, he learned to house the patients by selecting and distributing them according to their different illnesses and treatments. His ideal was: Through bodies, to souls!

And he became "the patriarch of charity", "the wonder of Granada", "the honor of his age". Today, he is considered "the creator of the modern hospital".

At the beginning of 1550, he fell gravely ill; a noble benefactress found him feverish on his poor bed, made of a bare tabletop, while the alms basket served him for a pillow. She obtained permission from the archbishop (which for John was the same as a command) to take him to her manor house. While they were taking him away, the poor were wailing and protesting, surrounding his stretcher, and John was distraught. He blessed them, weeping, and he said:

"God knows, my brothers, if I would like to die in your midst! But since He wants me to die without seeing you, may His will be done!"

In the too-soft bed, John revealed to the archbishop that he was distressed over three things:

"I have been negligent, even cowardly, in my service to God. I leave this life without being able to pledge assistance to the poor in my hospital and to the families who have looked to me for help. What will happen to them? There is another thing, too. This morning Anthony brought me a list of our debts. I was obliged to incur them, but I cannot pay them."

And saying this, he placed into his hands the register of the debts that he carried next to his heart. He had no peace until the archbishop pledged personally to settle them.

In the early dawn of March 8, when as yet there was no one around his bed, he got down from that too-comfortable mattress, knelt down on the floor clasping his crucifix to his chest, and expired at the age of fifty-five. That was how they found him, already dead for some time but still on his knees.

The funeral was lavish: the casket was carried by four gentlemen of the highest nobility, but at the front of the procession came the poor of his hospital.

Saint Camillus de Lellis
(1550–1614)

Born in Italy, in the same year in which the Portuguese John of God was dying in Spain, without knowing it, he inherited the same passion. He, too, was distressed by a stint at a Roman hospital for incurables, where the care was entrusted to mercenaries or to criminals on work release. He sought out companions inclined "to love the infirm Jesus Christ" and founded the Order of Clerks Regular, Ministers of the Infirm.

By his example, Camillus taught them Christian tenderness for the suffering, vigorously demanding that the whole hospital be impregnated with this, even in terms of practical management. At times he cried out to them: "More soul in the hands!"

And he often addressed the sick as if he were speaking heart to heart with Jesus Christ Himself.

He took over the hospitals of Naples, Milan, Genoa, Palermo, Bologna, and Mantua, and when he felt too old, he resigned from all positions of authority, asking to be able to reside and die in the hospital of the Holy Spirit in Rome.

To those who visited him he said, flustered with joy, "I am expecting good news from the Lord: Come, blessed of my Father, because I was infirm and you visited me."

He died at the age of sixty-four, but before this he had wanted to write a testament in order to leave his entire self as an inheritance. He had it signed by his friars and asked them to hang it around his neck, leaving it there even in the grave.

He had written:

> I, Camillus de Lellis. . . . leave my body of earth to the same earth where it was produced. I leave to the devil, the wicked tempter, all the sins and offenses that I have committed against God and for which I repent within the depth of my soul. . . . Item, I leave to the world all vanities and I desire to exchange this earthly life for the certainty of heaven, all of my stuff for eternal goods, all of my friends for the company of the saints, all of my relatives for the sweetness of the angels, and finally all worldly curiosities for the true vision of the face of God. Item, I leave and give my soul and every one of its powers to my beloved Jesus and to his Holy Mother and to my guardian angel. Item, I leave my will in the hands of the Virgin

Mary, Mother of Almighty God, and I intend not to will anything except that which the Queen of the Angels wills. Finally, I leave to Jesus Christ crucified all myself in soul and body, and I trust that, through His immense goodness and mercy, He may receive me and forgive me as He forgave the Magdalene and will be kind to me as He was to the good thief in the last moment of His life on the Cross.

In fact, he expired with a smile on his face just as the priest who was attending to him pronounced these words of the prayers for the dying: *Mitis atque festivus Christi Jesu tibi aspectus appareat* (May Christ show you His meek and merry face).

Saint Martín de Porres
(1579–1639)

Born in Lima, Peru, to a Spanish knight and a black former slave, to everyone he was only "a mulatto dog". He asked to enter the Dominican friars and was accepted as a lay brother, without the prospect of the priesthood. He was given the humblest offices, which he carried out with courage and gentleness. Because he had picked up some medical knowledge in the chambers of a barber surgeon, they allowed him to open a sort of clinic where he attended to the poor in particular, caring for them with unsurpassable tenderness and overcoming all repugnance. There were also miracles of healing. In Lima, they ended up calling him "Martin of charity".

Venerated even by the noble and the rich, he received many donations, with which he was able to found El Asilo de Santa Cruz, the first boarding school anywhere in the New World, intended for the abandoned children of the city. And Martín guaranteed not only the necessary support, but the presence of salaried assistants and educators. The girls were even guaranteed an appropriate dowry for when they reached marriageable age. It was in this way that —through the holy hands of the lowly mulatto friar—part of the wealth plundered by the mighty went back to the poor.

By the age of sixty, he was so debilitated they forced him to occupy, reluctantly, one of the beds of his infirmary and to stretch himself out on beautiful, clean white sheets.

The viceroy hurried over to kiss the hands of the dying mulatto, but he had to wait because (as Fray Martín explained) "He had to visit with the Holy Virgin and with Saint Dominic and some of the angels who had come to attend to him."

On that last evening of his life, as soon as his fellow friars had finished singing, according to the Dominican custom, the Salve Regina and the Credo, Fray Martín expired, while on the street—as the reports afterward stated—"all of Lima had gathered" to weep for him.

At the funeral, the viceroy, the archbishop of the city, the bishop of Cuzco, and the judge of the royal court insisted on carrying the casket.

This, too, can happen in the Church of God: the gap of social inequalities can be bridged by holiness. To the point that, in his country, *Fray Martín de la caridad* has been proclaimed patron of social justice.

Saint Peter Claver
(1580–1654)

Born in Catalonia, he was educated at the Jesuit boarding school, where he had the fortune of meeting the elderly saint Alphonsus Rodriguez (a doorkeeper, but a true spiritual master), who repeated to him: "The souls of the Indians have an infinite value, because they have the same price as the blood of Christ. . . . Go to the Indies to purchase all those souls that are being lost!"

So he got permission to go as a missionary to Colombia, to Cartagena (a major port for the unloading and selling of slaves), when he had not yet been ordained a priest. Here he made a vow to "dedicate his whole life to the conversion of the blacks" and began to sign his name like this: Peter Claver, slave of the Ethiopians forever.

On their behalf, he carried out a grueling ministry for forty years, baptizing roughly three hundred thousand of them. He would go to meet the ships of the slave traders that were coming into the port, on a boat loaded with basic necessities: disinfectants, bandages, food, lemons, tobacco, distilled spirits. And he immediately began to take care of the dying and the children. Then, when he had familiarized himself with those poor wretches, he began his catechesis, using big placards he had designed himself, to recount the Gospel and explain the principal truths of the Christian faith. He took care of the slaves and protected them in every way possible, and everyone recognized him as an undisputed spiritual authority, which made it possible for him to intervene even with the slave owners, correcting, resolving disputes, demanding justice.

He fell ill during the plague that broke out in Cartagena in 1650, and afterward he was tremendously weakened, in part because of his advanced age. Sad to say, he was not given much care. At times he did not even have enough food or other necessities. He took refuge in his poor cell, and there he remained, alone and happy, even though he was forgotten by all.

In his youth, he had been very unsure whether God

wanted him for the mission or for a hidden life of prayer. Now he could also satisfy that old contemplative vocation. He had with him a little handwritten notebook in which his old friend Brother Alphonsus Rodriguez had summarized for him the main maxims of the interior life. He read it and reread it, and it seemed to him that he was in paradise. He remained in these conditions of solitude and abandonment for many months.

The city seemed to reawaken and remember him only when the news spread that Father Peter had received the last sacraments: then everyone wanted to visit the Father; everyone hoped to get at least a relic of him. There was a crowd of nobles, of officials, of religious and priests. The gates of the friary were locked for the sake of prudence, but the crowd knocked them down. Then came waves of children who were already acclaiming Peter Claver as a saint, and in their wake there arrived an endless procession of Blacks, who forced their way to the cell of their benefactor.

When the body was displayed in church so everyone could kiss his hands without all the pushing and stumbling, they laid his arms out in the form of a cross. So he took on the beautiful crucified form he had always loved, offered, and desired.

He was proclaimed *universal patron of missions among the Black populations.*

Saint Vincent de Paul
(1581–1660)

Born to a family in humble circumstances, he spent his youth in an all-out effort to redeem himself socially, even embarking on the path of the priesthood for this purpose. One day, however, he had the grace to understand that the poor and poverty were his true riches. And there were two crises, above all, that tore at his heart: the lack of truly missionary priests and the huge segments of social poverty. For this reason, he founded the Congregation of the Mission to reevangelize the countryside. He then created a Company of the Daughters of Charity, furnished with the appropriate regulations, in such a way that assistance for the poor could be simultaneously generous and intelligent.

Assisted by the young widow Louise de Marillac, he took on the responsibility of caring for the hundreds of patients of the *Hôtel-Dieu* who were languishing in neglect; then for foundlings; then for prisoners and convicts; then for soldiers wounded on the battlefield; then for the beggars, elderly, crippled, and insane who were crowded into the outskirts of Paris.

In practice, Vincent became a sort of "minister of the poor", with quite a bit of influence at court. This made it possible for him to fight against the plan for the "great detention", which would have brought the forced hospitalization of all the beggars, the homeless, the jobless. Vincent, instead, wanted efforts to be aimed at the reintegration of the excluded, creating "centers of rehabilitation for work" for unemployed elderly craftsmen and setting up "little houses" to make it possible for beggars to maintain their family relations.

In this way, he demonstrated, with his astonishing sense of enterprise, that indeed "charity is infinitely creative."

He died with the name of Jesus on his lips, at the age of seventy-nine, after having practiced to the full what he had taught to his priests: "Let us love God, my brothers, but let us love Him at our own expense, with the toil of our arms, with the sweat of our brow." In France he was venerated as "Father of the Country".

Saint Giuseppe Benedetto Cottolengo
(1786–1842)

Trained for an ecclesiastical career from his youth, at the age of forty-one he had not given evidence of any particular virtue, but that all changed the night he was called to the side of a feverish mother of five who, having been turned away by all the hospitals, was dying in childbirth in a stable.

In anguish, he immersed himself in prayer: "My God, why? Why did you want me to witness this? What do you want from me?"

He came away completely changed and sure of one thing: "The grace is done! Blessed be our holy Lady!" He was to live for fifteen more years, and these were rich with breathtaking diligence. He started by founding a Little House of Divine Providence (little before God, but immense in the plans and dreams of the founder), intended for patients nobody wanted.

Cottolengo's genius was that of designing each residence to operate as a household: according to the patient (disabled and elderly, orphaned, mentally ill, blind, deaf-mute, or other), he sought to build for them a little "family" where they would not lack for assistants, doctors, teachers, administrators, managers.

He looked for the right kind of coworkers, and he got them! There was also no lack of the necessary structures (bakery, butcher shop, carpenter's shop, workshops of various kinds). If the participants then wanted to join permanently, this gave rise to the different religious congregations. And since it was also absolutely necessary to keep alive, for the good of all, "a heart engaged in intercession and in the worship of God", Cottolengo also became the founder of five monasteries of contemplative nuns and a monastery of hermits.

But he continued to call himself always and only "the laborer of Divine Providence".

The malicious said the canon had built a "poor town" around the outskirts of Turin. And he humorously called his work "my Noah's Ark". But there were those—surprised by such creative genius—who instead suggested the title of "university of Christian charity".

He died in 1842, with these words on his lips:

"*Misericordia, Domine! Misericordia, Domine!* Good and holy Providence! Holy Virgin, . . . now it's up to You!"

Saint Luigi Orione
(1872–1940)

He was born in Tortona to a very humble family, where he acquired a passion for labor and resistance to fatigue, together with a true zeal for the poor.

He was very young when he entered the seminary in Tortona, where he earned his keep by working as a sacristan at the cathedral, with permission to live in a few little rooms above the dome. He would bring street urchins there to teach them a bit of catechism and let them play hide-and-seek in the vast attic spaces.

Right after he was ordained a priest, he started the Little Work of Divine Providence, founding a farming cooperative for young men with no means for getting an education.

At the same time, he founded the Hermits of Divine

Providence, gathering in various communal houses (in Piedmont, Lombardy, Umbria, Lazio, Sicily) laymen accustomed to field work who wanted to consecrate themselves to the Lord in the Benedictine style.

In 1909, he organized assistance for the victims of the earthquake in Messina, and in 1915, he took care of children who had been orphaned by the Marsica earthquake in Abruzzo.

Starting in 1915, he began to open, all over Italy, nursing homes called Piccoli Cottolengo for people in the most repugnant conditions. That same year he founded the Little Missionary Sisters of Charity, as the women's branch of all his works. In 1927, he founded a congregation of visually handicapped sisters (the Blind Sacramentines) for perpetual Eucharistic adoration, asking them to be the prayerful heart of all the other works.

In March of 1940, after two heart attacks aggravated by respiratory crises, he was persuaded to take a few days of rest in the house founded in Sanremo, but he was uneasy, because even after all unnecessary furniture had been taken out of the room, it still seemed too luxurious! He said: "It is not among palm trees that I want to live and die, but among the poor who are Jesus Christ."

And he pleaded with the brother who was assisting him: "It doesn't feel right, I can't stay here: for pity's sake, look at the train schedule!"

Fortunately, in a corner there was a statuette of Our Lady, and then he calmed down:

"Look how beautiful she is!" he said. "Doesn't it seem to you that all I have to do is close my eyes?"

He closed them three days later, saying:

"Jesus, Jesus. I am going!"

For the last time he felt sent on mission, ready to give

swift obedience. At his death, the various branches of the Little Work of Divine Providence already numbered about 820 religious men and several hundred sisters, in a hundred or so foundations spread over many countries throughout the world.

Saint Damien De Veuster
(1840–1889)

He was a missionary originally from Belgium who had volunteered to live in Molokai, a remote and appalling island of Hawaii populated exclusively by lepers and referred to as "a living hell".

But at the news of his death, which took place in 1889, the *Times* was already writing: "This Catholic priest has become the friend of all humanity." And a Hawaiian newspaper was already calling him "a Christian hero".

From the first day he arrived on the island (where no white man had ever set foot), he had addressed those unfortunate people with the expression "we lepers" and had overcome the terrible wall that divided him from them (considered "untouchables") simply by accepting to be embraced, sharing with them the same table and the same food, tending to and bandaging with tenderness their repulsive wounds, working with them.

For their sake, he became architect, excavator, bricklayer, carpenter, involving them in the construction of chapels, homes, clinics, hospitals, warehouses, aqueducts, pharmacies, and orphanages.

But, above all, he rebuilt the sacred humanity of his patients, starting with assistance for the dying, bringing dignity to the funerals, seeing to the attentive and joyful celebration of the Christian feast days (he made Corpus Christi the most beautiful and moving feast of the island), and incorporating the sick into confraternities, genuine structures of coexistence and civil service.

To one who urged him to avoid contagion, he responded, "My son, if the disease takes away my body, God will give me another one!"

And when he contracted leprosy, paraphrasing Saint Paul, he said, "I have become a leper among the lepers in order to win them all for Christ."

But his identification with the poor lepers was not yet complete: the greatest suffering for Father Damien was that of having to die knowing that a letter had appeared in the international press, written by a Protestant pastor (jealous of his fame): "The simple truth is, he was a coarse, dirty man, headstrong and bigoted. . . . He was not a pure man in his relations with women, and the leprosy of which he died should be attributed to his vices and carelessness."

And he offered as evidence the vulgar persuasion that leprosy was a curse from God and the pseudo-scientific presupposition that saw it as akin to syphilis.

Father Damien's heart was broken, and yet he found the energy to write: "I will see to climbing very sweetly the way of the cross, and I hope to find myself soon at the summit of my Golgotha."

In 1959, when Hawaii became the fiftieth state of the United States of America, it had the right—on the basis of federal law—to place two statues of their illustrious figures on Capitol Hill in Washington: The first was that of one of their kings (a hero of the Hawaiian nation), the second was that of Father Damien.

Saint Albert Chmielowski
(1845–1916)

His baptismal name was Adam, and he became known in Warsaw as a brilliant and promising painter.

But his intense Christian faith kept bringing up in his soul the question: What is the purpose of art? What is the destiny of the artist?

For some time he had dedicated himself to the composition of an *Ecce Homo* (a canvas that would always remain incomplete) until he realized he would never succeed in creating the masterpiece of his dreams (it is now placed on his tomb) if he did not dedicate himself first to restoring in the poor the image of Christ suffering.

He wore a simple robe and had himself called Fratel Albert. He took care of some of the indigent, accommodating them in his own home, then decided to visit the homeless crowded into the public shelters in Kraków, where none but the poor ever dared to venture.

When he got inside, as soon as the poor men laid eyes on him, they threatened to kill him. And Chmielowski understood their misery was so extreme it could not be consoled or succored except on one condition: "It has to be by living with them! They cannot be left like that."

He sold all his paintings and went to live among them. Then, taking advantage of the summertime (when the shelters were empty), he had those awful poorhouses restored, renovated, and decorated, turning them into "houses of assistance". And he himself turned beggar for the sake of his destitute.

"Behold Adam Chmielowski—the one who used to be a famous painter—who has become father of the poor!"

the people said, when they saw him riding around the marketplace on an enormous wagon he had got custom-made for collecting donations: "He asked for alms with humility and with the sweetest smile and received offerings almost with tears of gratitude in his eyes. It was not clear who was happier, the one who received or the one who gave."

He had gathered many associates around him, eventually founding a congregation for men and one for women, both of which practiced absolute poverty: those wanting to enter had first to give to the poor all they possessed. And the people said the one going around the streets of Kraków was a new Saint Francis.

To his coworkers he explained, "I look at Jesus in His Eucharist—could His love have provided anything more beautiful? If He is bread, let us become bread, too, giving ourselves."

And he repeated tirelessly, "We must be good like bread!"

On December 23, 1916, he collapsed, worn out by a tumor that had been destroying his stomach for months. They laid him out on a bed slightly more comfortable than the cot he was used to sleeping on at the homeless shelter. When he came back to his senses, they heard him murmur, "What have you done to me, and where is this that you are pampering me? Give me back my cot and my straw pillow!"

He did not want to die away from his poor. And when they obeyed him, he said he finally felt right.

He died on Christmas Day, and there was an immense crowd at his funeral, led by all the civil and religious authorities. In his country they called him "the father of the poor".

Today the world honors him as "the Polish Saint Francis of the twentieth century".

One last word on the charity of the saints

When one contemplates the face of a saint of charity, and one reflects on the works he accomplished, the question arises of how a single human heart could have loved so much and dared so much. Even if one wanted to consider only the outward achievements (in terms of social enterprise, money employed, organization of resources, buildings constructed, coworkers involved, etc.), their work brings God into the picture, because it is not explainable without genuine miracles, for which, moreover, there is almost always abundant and indisputable documentation.

But there is one aspect that is too easily underappreciated: the saints of charity love the poor *because* they love Christ. They do not see Christ in the poor (almost exalting them). Instead, they see the poor in Christ. It is love for His *whole body* that makes them attentive to the suffering members.

And there is one test that clearly distinguishes these saints from all those Christians who instead idealize the poor, whether to put a bit of flesh on that Christ they consider abstract and far away or to gain for themselves, as believers, a certain "respect" from those who fight for the liberation of man.

These repeat at every step and in every circumstance: All that is done or not done for the poor, is done or refused to Christ.

The saints are certainly convinced of this, but they are even more persuaded of the "law of reversibility" that is included in this principle, on the basis of which all that is done for Christ is done for the poor.

The saints, therefore, when they honor Christ (with their prayers, with their actions, with their attentions, setting aside time and energy for Him), know they are also honoring the poor.

And when they defend Christ (His Church, His Word, His Law, His Pastors, His Gifts), they know they are also defending the poor.

And when they must choose between Christ and the poor (in certain circumstances and quandaries in which they find themselves on account of their humble and heartfelt adherence to the Church, to her authority and magisterium), they know choosing Christ will be to the benefit of the poor, while abandoning Him would sooner or later leave the poor abandoned, too.

This test of reversibility is needed above all today, given the increase in the numbers of Christians who use their "social charity" and their desire to serve the poor as a pretext for resentment against the Church (seen as too compromised with worldly power) and then against the faith itself (seen as alienating) or even against Christian morality (seen as not always binding).

And it cannot help but be worrying to note that often Christians do not grow in the faith with the same powerful drive with which they think they have grown in charity.

As has been seen in these last two chapters dedicated to workers of mercy, the saint who has had the greatest influence on the story of other saints has been Saint Vincent de Paul.

But when we speak of his boundless charity, we must not forget that one supreme form of charity was the insistent fight he waged for years against the rampant heresy of Jansenism and to get the pope to condemn it. The man, who was entirely immersed in questions of charity, considered even more decisive the questions relative to the defense of the true faith.

True charity, in fact, is born from the gaze that is never distracted, not even for a moment, from its focus on Jesus alive, recognized, and beloved, so much so that Vincent always insisted: "The main purpose for which God has called us is to love Our Lord Jesus Christ. If we depart even slightly from the thought that the poor are the members of Jesus Christ, without fail we will lose sweetness and charity."

Henri Brémond, the great historian of Christian spirituality, wisely pointed out: "It was not love for men that led Vincent to holiness, but rather holiness that made him truly and effectively charitable; it was not the poor who gave him to God, but it is God, on the contrary, who gave him to the poor."[1]

So there to mark the difference between charity and every other form of philanthropy, no matter how Christian it may be, are the saints, they who die filled with desire to meet at last that Jesus whom they have loved so much.

---

[1] Cited by Pope St. John Paul II in the homily for the 250th anniversary of his canonization (September 27, 1987).

CHAPTER VI

Dying of Apostolic Toil

The title of this chapter—dedicated to the saints who were priests and teachers in the faith—takes its cue from the teaching Saint Leopold Mandić gave to his students of theology when he was their educator during the first years of his ministry, "A priest must die of apostolic toil; there is no other death worthy of a priest."

A piece of advice he repeated to his fellow Capuchins gathered around him to celebrate the fiftieth anniversary of his priesthood, "Allow an old confrere to say a word to you: we are born for toil. It is a supreme joy to have the chance to busy ourselves with it. Let us ask God our Master that we may die of apostolic toil."

In the previous chapters, we linked the theme of holiness with that of charity. This is necessary because in Christianity charity necessarily flows from the heart of revelation: "God is love" and He wills that we should "abide in love" (1 Jn 4:16). Charity toward God and toward neighbor is, therefore, the first truth that must be affirmed and practiced.

This applies to all the saints and, therefore, to priests as well.

But the entirely special dedication of these latter to the ministry of the Word (in study, in preaching, and in mission) reminds us that if *the truth of charity* is necessary, even more necessary is *the charity of truth*: precisely that of those who are bound to teach, communicate, and defend the Truth that God has revealed to us, above all, about Himself.

Always (and particularly in certain eras) in order truly to defend charity, one must first of all defend the faith.

In the first Christian centuries, it was not charity toward one's neighbor that was put in danger, but faith in the revelation of the Trinity: that first truth which allows us to define *charity* as the very nature of God and the substantial love that sets the Divine Persons in relationship with each other and is extended to us.

And the same thing happens today, in many places and circumstances, when the standard of charity is brandished in order to conceal aggression against the truth.

We certainly cannot forget the immense and courageous charity with which the saints who died of apostolic toil expended their lives in the exercise of the priestly ministry, but we would like to emphasize above all the charity of their intelligence, with which they were able to defend and communicate the faith.

It is therefore right to begin by remembering that Father of the Church who strenuously defended faith in the Trinity (and therefore charity itself) in a West that the emperor Constantius II was forcing to become Arian (which meant denying the divinity of Christ).

Saint Hilary of Poitiers
DOCTOR AND FATHER OF THE CHURCH
(ca. 315–368)

From a prosperous family, he had converted to Christianity as a young man, renouncing "the sweet sensualism of leisure and wealth".

Elected bishop of Poitiers in the year 350, he was one of the first and greatest Doctors of the Church. In preaching and writing, he tenaciously defended the divinity of the Son of God against those heretics (called Arians because they were followers of the Alexandrian priest Arius) who maintained that, in spite of being the most perfect and foremost in dignity, He was a creature like all the rest. The situation was grave because Emperor Constantius had embraced the heresy and was seeking to impose it on all his subjects by force.

Because of this, Hilary had to undergo five years of exile in Asia Minor. He took advantage of this to learn Greek and to study all the great Fathers and Doctors of the Eastern Church. When he was able to go back to his country, he returned there with the masterpiece he had composed: a splendid treatise *On the Trinity* (the first in the Latin language), which was decisive for the Christians of the West. The heretics were presenting themselves as defenders of the Unicity of God, and there was something ingenious and stirring about their arguments: they maintained that the divine had to remain divine and the human had to remain human, otherwise some of the absoluteness and glory of God would be lost.

They therefore accepted that Jesus-as-Man who came from God to enlighten our world, but they rejected that

Jesus-as-God who came to reveal to us the divine world. Hilary, instead, passionately defended the whole truth of Christ: true Son of God, come to reveal to us that the divine nature is all Love, but a "communicative" love, shared by three Divine Persons (the Father, the Son, and the Holy Spirit) and mercifully open to receive all creatures in communion.

The most beautiful characteristic of Saint Hilary's treatise on the Trinity is that from start to finish it is a dialogue with God: "In it, reflection turns into prayer, and prayer comes back as reflection."

Hilary was able to bring the West back to the true faith, dialoguing with everyone, but he did so by combining strength with gentleness. After retiring to his diocese, he was able to dedicate himself to his beloved studies and to the composition of the earliest sacred hymns to have been preserved in the West.

And it was with the joyful knowledge that he was finally plunging into the ocean of divine love—of which he had spoken so much—that Hilary came to the end of his life in the year 368.

It is recounted that at the moment of his death, his room was flooded with a light so bright the eye was not able to endure it: a little miracle to remind those present of the immense light Hilary had given to the Church. He was considered and called a saint while he was still alive.

Saint Martin of Tours
BISHOP
(316–397)

He received baptism from Saint Hilary of Poitiers. Born in Hungary, Martin had followed in his father's footsteps, embracing a military career to the point of becoming part of the imperial guard. He has gone down in history for what he did on behalf of a beggar who was shivering with cold: he unsheathed his sword, cut in two the beautiful mantle of his uniform, and gave half of it to the poor man. That night Jesus appeared to him, covered with his half mantle, thanking him for his generosity and introducing him to his angels, saying, "This is Martin, who although not yet baptized has dressed me with his mantle." Finally the soldier had found his true Lord!

He left the military life and went to Poitiers to find Hilary (considered one of the most learned and holy men of the time) and to be instructed and baptized by him. Then Hilary became bishop of the city, and Martin built a hermitage on its outskirts, gathering a few disciples around him. It was the first "monastery" in the West. Invited on a pretext to go to the nearby city of Tours, he was elected bishop. He accepted, but continued to live together with other monks in a hermitage made of huts, dedicating himself to the tireless work of evangelizing the population of rural France, where he established numerous monastic centers. He led his diocese for twenty-seven years.

He died at the age of nearly eighty in Candes, where he had gone in an attempt to reconcile the local priests, who were divided into factions. During his last days, exhausted by toil and suffering, he wanted to die, but his prayer was: "Lord, if your people still need me, I do not refuse to suffer." Witnesses recounted that Martin's face continued to glow even after his death, as if surrounded by a light of glory. And next to his bed, a choir of angels was heard singing.

He was one of the most beloved saints of the Middle Ages. It is calculated that in France alone, more than four thousand churches have been dedicated to him. King Clovis I proclaimed him "protector of the king of the Franks and of the Frankish people".

Saint Ambrose

DOCTOR AND FATHER OF THE CHURCH

(ca. 340–397)

He had chosen the career of a magistrate—following in the footsteps of his father, the Roman prefect of Gaul—and at the age of thirty found himself already consul of Milan, the city that at the time was the capital of the empire. So on that December 7 of the year 374, when Catholics and Arians were fighting over the right to appoint the new bishop, it was up to him to guarantee public order in the city and prevent riots from breaking out. The unforeseeable happened when he spoke to the crowd with such good sense and authority that a cry went up: "Ambrose for bishop!" And to think that he was just a catechumen awaiting baptism! He gave in when he understood this, too, was the will of God, who wanted him in His service.

He started by distributing his belongings to the poor and dedicating himself to the systematic study of Sacred Scripture. He learned to preach, becoming one of the most celebrated orators of his time, capable of enchanting even a refined intellectual like Augustine of Hippo, who converted thanks to him. From Ambrose, the Church of Milan received an imprint that endures to this day, including in the field of liturgy and music. He kept good and close ties with the emperor, but was capable of resisting him when it was necessary, reminding all that "the emperor is within the Church, not above the Church." And when he learned that Theodosius the Great had ordered a violent and unjust repression in Thessalonica, he was not afraid to demand public expiation from the sovereign. He left his Church a rich treasury of teachings, above all, in the field of moral and social life.

He spent the last years of his life concerned like a father not only about his own diocese but also about the nearby Churches, where they usually called on him to bring peace. In Vercelli, where he was already feverish when he arrived, they said "he had lit up, like a ray of sunshine, the whole city." And he had begun to write a treatise *On the Goodness of Death*, in which he exhorted himself in the first place: "Let us hasten toward the Life, let us seek Him who lives!"

His death agony began on Good Friday of the year 397. In his *Life of Ambrose*, his secretary and biographer Paulinus recounts: "[In his last days] he had seen the Lord Jesus coming to him and smiling. . . . And right when he left us to fly to the Lord, from the fifth hour of the afternoon until the hour in which he gave up his soul, he prayed with his arms open in the form of a cross."

It was the early hours of Holy Saturday. And several young people who were filing past the dead body of Ambrose said they had seen a star shining on his forehead. Perhaps it is only a legend. But it is beautiful when young people recount that they have seen a star shining on the forehead of their bishop.

Saint Jerome

DOCTOR AND FATHER OF THE CHURCH

(ca. 342–420)

He was born in Stridon, in Dalmatia, to a Christian family. Sent to Rome to complete his studies, he fell in love with the pagan classics, which he studied doggedly, although he was not above indulging in the decadent life of students at the time.

At the age of nineteen, he was already in Trier, in the Rhineland, where the imperial court was situated, looking for a post worthy of his capabilities. Fortunately, he was also able to find time to explore further the faith he had neglected to that point, although he felt a certain repugnance at the ugly Latin into which the Sacred Scriptures had been translated.

He traveled to Greece and Asia Minor, but his decisive conversion took place during a serious illness. He dreamed he had come to the end of his life and had to undergo the judgment of God, but when he tried to present himself to the Supreme Judge as a Christian, he heard these words: "You are not a Christian, but a Ciceronian!"

He recovered, in body and soul, and the Bible became his only treasure. He studied Hebrew in order to be able to read the original codices, and he gradually became "the man of God's Word", deeply learned and deeply a believer.

He was thirty-five when his friend Pope Damasus suggested he revise the Latin translation of the Gospels, tracking down all the most ancient manuscripts in the original language. After the pope died, Jerome's enemies began to close in, and he fled to the Holy Land, establishing himself in Bethlehem, in a cave near that of the Nativity. Here he patiently translated into Latin all the other books of Scripture and thus realized the *Vulgata* (the official biblical text in use down to our own day).

He died in old age, exhausted by work, so much so that he said he felt like "a little old donkey that can't go on anymore". But his last writing (a letter sent from Bethlehem to the great Augustine) conveys the joy of one who feels the hour of rest drawing near and trembles with the desire finally to meet that Christ whom he had long sought and invoked in the sacred texts.

Saint Augustine of Hippo
DOCTOR AND FATHER OF THE CHURCH
(354–430)

He was born in Thagaste in 354. He learned about the Christian faith in his childhood but did not receive baptism. As a youth, he let himself be drawn in by the humanistic aspects of paganism. He formed a bond with a woman of a lower class, with an impassioned and faithful love, although he knew that (according to the laws of the time) he could not marry her. He dedicated himself to classical studies and got a position teaching rhetoric in Milan. There he met Saint Ambrose, who fascinated him by the beauty with which he explained the Sacred Scriptures.

Finally, at the Easter vigil in 387, he received baptism. On the way back home with his mother, Monica, they stopped in Ostia, where she died a holy death.

When he got to Thagaste, he withdrew to a little monastery of laymen to devote himself to painstaking meditation on the Sacred Scriptures. He was pulled away from this refuge by the bishop of Hippo, who wanted at all costs to consecrate him as a priest.

In 395, Augustine succeeded him in the episcopate. In addition to his celebrated *Confessions*, his numerous *Treatises* are also famous, in particular those on the primacy of God's grace in the work of salvation and on the reasonableness of the faith. Augustine said: "You must understand in order to believe", but also: "You must believe in order to understand."

And he saw in the Church the good Mother who keeps watch over the "yes" of believers. Finally, he also described the mystery of the *City of God*, in which there coexist those who want to love God above all things and those who above all else love themselves.

"And the two loves give rise to two cities that, however, overlap each other": the city of God is therefore subject to the vicissitudes of history, but it is indestructible because it is built on true love. When he finished writing this "great and arduous" work, he was seventy-two years old.

Meanwhile, a barbarian horde was threatening to spill over from Spain onto the coasts of Africa as well.

During the few years he still had left, while he continued tirelessly to write new theological works, he was forced to witness the systematic destruction of all the flourishing African churches by the Vandals. In the end, the church in Hippo was one of only three remaining, and the city— in which many other bishops had taken refuge—was besieged.

After three months of siege, the great old man fell ill: he stayed in his poor quarters living out those "most bitter" last days, praying to God and offering Him his life. He had had the penitential Psalms written down for him on big sheets of parchment and attached to the walls so he could always recite them. He asked forgiveness for himself and for all, "and he continually wept hot tears." He said: "I am not afraid of dying, because we have a good Lord." He had asked that no one be let into his room anymore, because he wanted to spend his last days alone with God.

He died at the age of seventy-six, leaving the Church an immense inheritance: his monasteries and his books, all impregnated with passion for the Holy Trinity. He had written in his *Confessions*: "A body tends by its weight towards the place proper to it. . . . Fire tends upwards, stone downwards. . . . My weight is my love (*Pondus meum amor*

meus): Wherever I go, my love is what brings me there"
(13,9,10).[1]

Saint Benedict of Nursia

PATRON OF EUROPE AND FATHER OF MONASTICISM

(ca. 480–547)

Born in Nursia, he spent his youth in Rome. But feeling nauseated by the corrupt life that was led there, he felt the desire for an existence devoted to prayer and solitude.

"Desiring to please only God, wisely ignorant and wisely unlearned", he withdrew at first to Subiaco, then tried to lead a community of monks in Vicovaro, but in the end he preferred solitude even more, although he allowed a few hermits to put themselves under his guidance.

In 529, he built, in the area of Cassino, a genuine monastery according to an ideal he expressed in the *Rule*, in which discipline is always tempered with charity. In it the monastery is conceived of as "a school for learning to serve the Lord" ("without ever placing anything before the love of Christ") in such a way as to be able to become "the fundamental cell of a new society".

Ora et labora was and remains the Benedictine ideal: to carry out "the work of God" by means of prayer lived as work, and of work lived as a prayer, in a unity aimed at fostering desire for God and attention to beauty in the liturgy, in work, in love for letters.

In this way, the abbey of Montecassino became the prototype of a thousand others spread all over Europe and, at

---

[1] Augustine, *Confessions*, trans. F. J. Sheed, 2nd ed. (Indianapolis and Cambridge: Hackett, 2006), pp. 294–95.

the time of the barbarian invasions, would save the heritage of classical culture and develop a true Christian humanism.

Benedict was just over the age of sixty when God gave him the last gift: one night he was praying silently, standing at the window, when a light slowly began to spread until everything seemed to shine as in broad daylight. And "during this vision, a miraculous thing happened, as he himself would say afterward: before his eyes the whole world presented itself as gathered together beneath a single ray of sunshine."

Even Saint Gregory the Great, who recounts this conclusive episode, struggles to explain the meaning and the very possibility of such a vision. In any case, he explains it like this: "It was not earth and heaven that shrank, it was the soul of the visionary that expanded."

And this is a recurrent note in the experience of many saints, which deserves to be emphasized: the last prayer, the last vision, concerns God the Creator and the beauty of all creatures. The first article of the Credo is also the last truth to be fully believed and savored.

By this time, the holy patriarch knew he had come to the end of his journey. He had himself brought to the oratory of the monastery, received the Eucharist, and then "with the help of his disciples who were holding up his weak members, he remained standing with his hands lifted up to heaven until he expired, murmuring a last prayer."

He died as he had lived, in the position of prayer, while some of the monks in monasteries far away received the vision of a road, entirely covered with rugs, that went straight up to heaven, toward the east, and a voice explained to them: "This is the way by which Benedict, dear to God, has ascended to heaven."

Saint Anselm of Canterbury
BISHOP AND DOCTOR OF THE CHURCH

(ca. 1033–1109)

He was born to a family related to the House of Savoy. Reacting to pressure from his father to get involved in the family business, he ran away from home, making his way to the abbey of Le Bec in Normandy, one of the most flourishing schools of theology at the time, led by Abbot Lanfranc. Here he completed his studies up to the priesthood, earning esteem through his qualities of mind and heart.

In 1078, Lanfranc was elected to the episcopal see of Canterbury, and Anselm, still rather young, was appointed abbot. He did not, however, neglect his philosophical and theological studies, and became one of the most prolific religious authors of his time.

In 1092, he again succeeded Lanfranc in the archepiscopal see, becoming primate of England. But he clashed with the ambitions of King William the Red, who repeatedly forced him into exile. The dispute hinged upon the freedom of the Church and also continued under Henry I. But he was able to combine goodness with firmness and daring and finally succeeded in winning the sovereign's trust.

Together with Saint Augustine and Saint Thomas Aquinas, Anselm is considered one of the greatest theologians of the Western Church.

He has left us treatises on God, whose existence is proven by the fact that there must necessarily exist "the Being than which nothing greater can be conceived". He also wrote a treatise entitled *Why Did God Become Man?* And he is the source of the famous and wise principle: "Faith requires the work of reason." One beautiful characteristic of his theology is the fact that it often turns into prayer.

His death was marked by a sweet coincidence. We know, in fact, from his biographer Eadmer that as a child Anselm had imagined "that the dwelling place of the good God was amid the high and snowy peaks of the Alps, at the foot of which he lived. One night he dreamed he was invited to this splendid palace by God himself, who visited with him affably and at length, and finally offered him the whitest bread to eat."

So then, the saint died after listening to the gospel of the daily Mass in which Jesus said: "As my Father appointed a kingdom for me, so do I appoint for you that you may eat and drink at my table" (Lk 22:28).

Saint Bernard of Clairvaux
FATHER AND DOCTOR OF THE CHURCH
(1090–1153)

More precisely, he is considered the last of the great Fathers of the Church and the first of her modern Doctors. And he is also one of the greatest saints of the second millennium: he is situated right at the beginning of it and would influence it profoundly.

He was born in Fontaines, near Dijon, in the years in which—as a reaction against the opulence of the Benedictines of Cluny—the Cistercian Reform had been born, with a poor remote monastery out in the marshes of Cîteaux. But the experiment was not very successful and seemed destined to come to an end. And this is what would have happened if, on Easter morning of 1112, Bernard had not come to the gates at the head of a band of thirty young men, companions of chivalrous adventures (including four brothers and two uncles). On his own, he had gathered them for six months in a castle to lead a communal life under his leadership: he had patiently got them to fall in love with Christ and His Church, convincing them little by little to choose the poorest form of monastic life then in existence.

After just three years of austere and pious life spent in Cîteaux, Bernard was chosen as founder of Clairvaux along with twelve other monks. This began his long career as an abbot, which would last for thirty-eight years, during which he would found a good sixty-eight monasteries.

Many legends connected to his Marian devotion and his *oratio ignata* (fired-up prayer) find historical support in his extraordinary talent in preaching and, above all, in his prayer. In both speech and writing, Bernard used a language that seemed directly drawn from Scripture, as if he had learned to talk from this alone.

Because of his great authority and holiness, he was forced to intervene in the most serious problems of the Church of his time, which in 1130 was divided between Pope Innocent II and the antipope Anacletus II.

He traveled around Europe to advance the recognition of the true pope and to restore the unity that had been damaged. In 1140, he debated Abelard in public, berating him for the excessive rationalism of his theological inquiry. He was no less abrupt and severe with Arnold of Brescia, a political-religious agitator.

His influence grew even more when in 1145 the pontificate went to one of his disciples, Blessed Eugene III, whom he did not deprive of the abundance of his fatherly counsel.

His travels in keeping tabs on his monasteries and in preaching, the toil of composing a great number of letters and various writings, the schedule and austerity that he imposed upon himself all wore him out.

His works had more influence, a reach more thorough and more prolonged over time than any other Christian (even Augustine) ever had.

But perhaps the influence he exercised over the Christian people will become clearer to us if we recall that it is precisely to this "doctor with the word sweet as honey"—as he is traditionally called—that we owe the development of the popular devotion to the holy Humanity of Christ.

He is the originator, in fact, of the habit dear to many Christians of meditating on the mysteries of the Nativity, on the sufferings of the Passion of Christ, on the joys and sorrows of the Mother of Jesus.

Rightly, in the stained glass of the basilica of Issoudun, an anonymous artist decided to illustrate the significance of the experience and message of our white-clad abbot with this image: the saint stands in front of his divine Teacher, but in Bernard's heart is written *Jesus* and in the heart of Jesus is written *Bernard*.

He is considered "the father of European sentiment".

Saint Dominic de Guzmán
FOUNDER
(1170–1221)

He was born in Caleruega, in Old Castile. After beginning his studies, he brilliantly completed the whole curriculum of philosophy and theology, becoming a canon of the cathedral of Osma, one of the oldest and most prestigious bishoprics of Spain. Accompanying his bishop on a journey to the lands of the North, he felt drawn to a missionary vocation. He

went to Rome to ask the pope for authorization to evange-
lize the Nordic tribes, but the pontiff, instead, assigned him
to the south of France, devastated by the Cathar heresy.

Dominic therefore began to travel through those lands,
in humility and poverty, like a "solitary pilgrim of Christ".
This gave him the idea of founding an *Order of Preachers* that
would be able to unite the "grace of preaching" (and therefore study and scholarship) with a poor and evangelical way
of life. He gave his friars *Constitutions* that to this day are
considered a masterpiece of juridical wisdom. He spent the
last years of his life dedicated only to "either speaking with
God or speaking about God".

At the end of July in 1221, exhausted by apostolic toil,
he was taken to the biggest friary of the order, which at
the time was the one in Bologna, where, however, he had
neither a room nor a bed. Only a cot made of rope, in a
corner.

On August 6—feast of the Transfiguration—he wanted
the friars to be gathered around his cot so he could give
them his last admonitions, insisting in a heartfelt and severe
manner on poverty. He then said he wanted to be buried
"under the feet of his friars": certainly out of humility, perhaps also in order to remain as their support. He himself
led the prayers for the commendation of the soul, then entrusted all of those present to the Father of heaven, repeating the same words that Jesus spoke on the last evening of
his life: "Those you gave me I have kept for you. Now I
commend them to you again in turn: preserve and protect
them!" He expired transfigured, even if he was dressed in
a habit so old and tattered they had to find another for him
so his body could be displayed in a dignified manner.

The friars, meanwhile, studied that face hollowed out
by suffering and by passion, but still innocent like that of a

child, and they must have thought with tenderness of the last confidence the Father had shared with them before he died —over which he had some misgivings ("perhaps I should not have said it!" he had whispered afterward)—revealing all the childlike candor of his spirit, "I have not succeeded in avoiding the imperfection of feeling more attraction in conversing with young women than with those of advanced age."

For his young friars, he would have desired even that ultimate purity which he had not succeeded in attaining.

Saint Albert the Great
DOCTOR OF THE CHURCH
(1206–1280)

He was born in Bavaria to a noble family. After studying at the University of Padua, he entered the Dominicans and was immediately called to teach at the universities of Cologne and Paris. The expertise of his writings ranged from Sacred Scripture (which he commented on in its entirety) to mysticism, from philosophy to theology, from astronomy to physics, from chemistry to mineralogy, from botany to medicine, from anthropology to zoology, always defending the right autonomy of reason in experimental research (and because of this he has also been proclaimed patron of scientists).

Pope Benedict XVI said of him: "Saint Albert the Great reminds us that there is friendship between science and faith and that through their vocation to the study of nature, scientists can take an authentic and fascinating path of holiness."[2]

[2] Benedict XVI, General Audience, Wednesday, March 24, 2010.

147 OF APOSTOLIC TOIL

His last years and his death took place as the holy Virgin had foretold to him in his youth. Here is the account of it taken from the *Legenda Coloniensis* (an anonymous chronicle written in the fifteenth century):

> It happened one day that the blessed Father Albert, already bent with years, stood as usual at his podium in the friary of Cologne, giving a talk in front of a large and illustrious audience. All of a sudden, he seemed to be having trouble putting together the arguments to demonstrate his thesis: his memory began to fail him, to the great astonishment of all. After a silent pause he recovered from the disturbance and said:
>
> "My dear ones [. . .] when as a young man I devoted myself to study [. . .] I often implored with tears and sighs the sweet and compassionate Virgin and ardently beseeched her to give me the light of eternal wisdom and at the same time to strengthen my heart in the faith, so that I would never go astray on account of the philosophical sciences. . . . She appeared to me and consoled me with these words: 'Persevere, my son, in study, because God will safeguard your science and will keep it pure for the good of the Church. But so that you may never waver in your faith, all your art of reasoning will be taken from you at the end of your life. You will become again like a child, through the innocence and candor of your faith; then you will go to God. And when one day it happens that you lose your memory during a public lecture, this will be the sign that your judge is about to visit you.' My dear ones, behold: today is fulfilled what was announced to me."
>
> Then he renewed his profession of faith, asked forgiveness for any imprecision in the things he had said or taught, and weeping humbly came down from the podium.

That which sooner or later happens to almost all the elderly, who one day suddenly feel their minds wavering and their powers diminishing, is here recounted in a mystical vein, as an appointment with the Mother who delivers back to God a son who has returned to being a child but is ready for his definitive birth into life.

Albert, therefore, died *in dulcedine societatis* (in the sweetness of fraternal communion), surrounded by friends and disciples, on November 15, 1280.

There was, however, this uniquely holy aspect: that he—to whom his contemporaries gave the title of "great" and his posterity that of "universal doctor" (Albert's *Opera Omnia* run to forty volumes)—maintained the candor of innocence even in the most prestigious university posts.

Saint Thomas Aquinas
DOCTOR OF THE CHURCH
(1225–1274)

Thomas was born in Roccasecca di Aquino to a family related to the principal ruling houses of Europe. As a child, he was brought up at the abbey of Montecassino, but the young man was attracted to study and obtained permission to attend the University of Naples. Here he got to know the Dominicans and joined that new order of mendicant friars. His family reacted harshly, having Thomas kidnapped and imprisoned in a castle, where his brothers tried to dissuade him in every way they could. He succeeded in escaping, and his superiors sent him to the University of Cologne, to the school of Albert the Great. After this, he went to the University of Paris, where he became a Master in Theology. With the help of one of his fellow friars, who translated Aristotle from the Greek for him, he undertook the huge project of demonstrating the harmony between reason and faith, between philosophy and theology.

The most mature fruit of his studies was the *Summa theologiae*. In him, reflection was accompanied by contemplation, and contemplation was accompanied by the passion for transmitting to others the truths contemplated. It was Thomas who composed, with a burning heart, the precious Eucharistic hymns that are still used today in liturgical prayer.

It is recounted that one day, while he was prostrate in front of the crucifix, he heard a voice: "Thomas, you have written well of me. What recompense do you want?"

And he replied, "Nothing other than you, Lord!"

Three weeks before he died, during the celebration of the Mass, he had a mystical experience so intense that from that time on he no longer wanted to write. He confided to one of his fellow friars: "What I have written is only straw in comparison with what has been revealed to me."

Sent by the pope to the Council of Lyon, he fell ill during the trip and was put up in the Cistercian abbey of Fossanova. One tradition, presented in an inscription on a wall of the abbey, recounts that during his last days he gave in to the repeated insistence of his hosts, who were asking him for some reflections on the *Song of Songs*, in the manner of Saint Bernard.

When he came to the seventh chapter, Thomas ran across these words: "Come, my beloved, let us go into the garden . . ." "He read these with vehement ardor of the spirit and with supreme joy, and immediately gave up the soul . . . [which] left the mortal body for the garden of eternal happiness."

He was forty-nine years old. Afterward, when it had to be decided if he was to be proclaimed a saint, to those who objected that Thomas had not worked any miracles in his life, Pope John XXII replied:

"As many theological affirmations as he wrote, that's how many miracles he worked!"

He wanted to indicate the prodigious synthesis of intellect and love with which Thomas had composed his works.

And Thomas was acknowledged with the title of *Angelic Doctor*.

Saint Ignatius of Loyola
FOUNDER
(1491–1556)

He was a knight eager for love and glory and thought he would win them by defending Pamplona from a siege by the French. But a wound in his leg left him crippled. Immobilized in a long convalescence, Ignatius had spent the time reading romances of chivalry, but while recovering at Loyola he was given only a *Life of Christ* and a book of *Legends of the Saints*. He was amazed to realize that these, too, contained splendid adventures. "Why not me?" he began to ask himself. And he sought an explanation for an interior experience that surprised him: when he thought about earthly adventures, he was at first filled with joy, but then fell back into sadness; when, instead, he thought about imitating the saints, he was melancholy at first, but then his soul was filled with a lasting joy.

He decided to become a true "soldier of Jesus Christ". He went to the shrine of Montserrat and laid down his knightly clothing and arms before the holy Virgin. He became a pilgrim and penitent in Manresa and received special illuminations there. He wrote a brief but decisive book on the *Spiritual Exercises*, in order to help some of his friends on the interior journey. But he understood that first he had to undertake serious theology studies and become a priest.

He went to the University of Paris and gathered his first

six companions around him. Once they were ordained priests, they went to Rome to place themselves at the disposal of the pope, who gladly approved their obedient new Society [of Jesus].

After providing it with *Constitutions* of its own, Ignatius channeled its energies toward two fundamental areas: missionary proclamation in faraway countries and the cultural formation of the new Christian generations.

He died in 1556, but he had been waiting for death for at least five years on account of very serious health problems. He was not disturbed about this, but, on the contrary, in his *Autobiography* had revealed that "thinking about death, he felt such joy and such spiritual consolation at having to die that he dissolved entirely into tears. This became so habitual with him that he often stopped thinking about death so as not to feel so much of that consolation."[3]

He thus left this life in such simplicity and almost in solitude, "like an ordinary person, without the gestures one usually expects from a founder".

But when the news of his end spread in Rome, everyone immediately exclaimed: "The saint has died!"

Saint Francis Xavier

CO-PATRON OF THE MISSIONS

(1506–1552)

It was at the University of Paris that the young nobleman Francisco de Xavier had the fortune of meeting Saint Ignatius of Loyola.

"What does it profit a man to gain the whole world if he

---

[3] Ignatius of Loyola, *Autobiography*, trans. Father Parmananda Divarkar, in *The Spiritual Exercises and Selected Works*, ed. George E. Ganss, S.J. (New York and Mahwah, N.J.: Paulist Press, 1991), no. 33, p. 82.

then loses his soul?" Ignatius would repeat in the courtyards of the university, with the ardor of a convert.

And after resisting at first, Francis ended up becoming one of his most faithful disciples. It was to him that Ignatius entrusted the first great mission to the Indies, which the pope was requesting. He had been given the title of "Pontifical legate for the whole Far East", but Xavier left for those faraway lands knowing that on his own—devoid of all resources and of any real power—he had to "take possession of a whole quarter part of the world for the Cross of Christ". He had decided to begin with those deepest in poverty and began his ministry by proclaiming the Gospel to the pearl divers, on the southern tip of India, also protecting them from exploitation by the Portuguese merchants. Then he departed for the faraway Spice Islands (Celebes and New Guinea) to track down some recent converts who had been left to themselves.

In this way, he spent years in constant travels, but always feeling that he was in mission territory, because Francis looked at everyone he met as his responsibility, even a lone fisherman giving him a lift on his boat or a group of children playing in some remote village he was passing through. Meanwhile, the letters and accounts he was sending to Ignatius were making the rounds all over Europe, eliciting new missionary vocations. Francis finally decided to go to Japan, but he discovered that in order to guarantee a future for that mission, he had to begin by evangelizing China.

On the rocky little island of Sancian, a short distance from Canton, for days and days Francis waited for the junk of a Chinese smuggler who had promised to take him to his longed-for, mysterious China. He was staying in a straw hut, contemplating by turns the distant horizon and a crucifix they had placed beside him. When the date that had been set passed without any vessel appearing on the horizon, exhausted by hunger and cold and completely alone, he knew death was near. The prayers he had learned as a child came back to his lips, and once again he recited them in his mother tongue.

So this was how he died on December 3, 1552, entirely bent on an immense mission that he had not even been able to begin. But on that abandoned shore, the heart of the Church was already beating. And Francis would have died full of gratitude if he had known that, in faraway Italy, in Macerata, only two months before, the child had been born who would inherit his dream, his vocation, and his mission: the servant of God Matteo Ricci.

Saint Philip Neri

FOUNDER

(1515–1595)

He had been born in Florence and had grown up so easygoing and generous everyone called him *Pippo bòno*. Then he moved to Rome to study and became a tutor in the home of a Florentine banker. He was not a priest, but at times he helped (even in preaching) an elderly priest and often brought his own Christian testimony to the poor neighborhoods, the prisons, and the hospitals. He also had a passion for visiting the ancient Christian catacombs, where he immersed himself in prayer. In preparation for the jubilee of 1550, he founded a confraternity to assist the pilgrims who would come streaming into Rome.

He then agreed to be ordained a priest, but on the condition of maintaining a certain freedom. He took up residence in a little room at the church of Saint Jerome, where he invited friends, penitents, and above all boys seeking a good Christian education.

This was the start of the first Oratory in history, where—under Philip's leadership—meetings, conferences, and recreational and musical activities were held. One of his most famous and well-attended events was the carnival he organized as an alternative to the pagan licentiousness that was customary at the time.

Beginning in 1564, Philip became the focal point of a community of priests who wanted to live and work according to his style, with its excellent combination of humanity, holiness, and freedom. In Rome, Philip was famous for his sense of humor (often condensed in aphorisms, anecdotes, and jokes) that served as a serene and intelligent form of pedagogy. Philip was also very much sought out in the confessional, and the saint dedicated long hours to it day and night.

In 1592, it seemed Philip was about to die. The doctors had closed the curtains around his bed and told those present to wait in peace for the imminent end when all of a sudden everyone heard him exclaim:

"O my most holy Lady! My beautiful Lady! My blessed Lady!"

They opened the curtains and found him on his knees, with his hands raised, weeping and repeating:

"I am not worthy! Who am I, O my dear Lady, that you should come to me? Who am I? O most holy Virgin! O Mother of God! O blessed among women!"

When he awoke from that ecstasy, he said to those present:

"Did you not see the Mother of God, who came to visit me and to take away my sufferings?"

He was already seventy-seven years old, but he had three more years to live. And he spent them in continual prayer.

What he desired, more and more each day, was holy Communion. When he was unable to sleep, instead of having the doctor called, he asked, "Give me my Lord, and then I will fall asleep!"

He died at the age of eighty, after an illness of several months, saying he was suffering greatly but only because "Jesus got a Cross and he a clean and comfortable bed." They called him "the saint of Christian Joy".

Saint Charles Borromeo
BISHOP AND REFORMER
(1538–1584)

He was one of the main theologians and bishops of the Catholic Counter-Reformation of the sixteenth century. Born in Arona to a noble family, he studied law in Pavia, graduating with great distinction at the age of just twenty-one. Although he was not a priest, he was immediately made cardinal-dean by his uncle Giovanni Angelo Medici, just elected pope with the name Pius IV, who chose him as his secretary of state.

When the work of the Council of Trent concluded in 1563, Charles was ordained a priest and bishop and decided to dedicate himself completely to the pastoral care of the diocese of Milan. In order to implement the necessary reforms there, he celebrated six provincial councils and eleven diocesan synods. He visited it a number of times, getting to even the most distant parishes and leaving indelible traces of his holy passage as a reformer.

He founded the Confraternity of Christian Doctrine and the Confraternities of the Most Holy Sacrament and of the

Rosary. He promoted the establishment of the Mounts of Piety.

Above all, he created seminaries to guarantee the formation of a new and holy clergy. He restored the ancient Ambrosian Rite in the Milanese Church. In the famine of 1570 and the subsequent terrible plague of 1576, he spared no effort in organizing aid and assistance for the needy and sick, donating all the fabric, even the most expensive, kept in the cupboards of the archbishop's residence so it could be made into clothing and blankets for the sick. He even had all the silver sold, and he sent to the isolation hospital even his own poor bed.

He lived in continual penance, so much so that—from every quarter—he was sent appeals to moderation and even the pope sent him a brief (an official document, no less) requiring him to take care of himself.

But to those who chastised him for his excessive penance, Charles responded:

"In order to give light to others, the candle has to consume itself. . . . That is what we should do."

He died at the age of forty-six, after a brief death agony spent contemplating with great emotion the paintings in his room of the Passion of Christ, which he had had placed around his bed.

His last words were: "Look, Lord, I am coming . . ."

When in the late evening of November 3, 1584, the tolling of the passing bell came from high up on the cathedral, the square of the archbishop's residence was flooded with people: men, women, children, priests, and religious were trying to push their way into the house to be with their father and pastor. Everyone wanted "to see the saint".

Even the civil authorities sent their condolences to the pope, stating (these were their exact words) that Charles had been able to acquire for himself, in Milan, "an incredible love".

Saint Francis de Sales

BISHOP AND DOCTOR OF THE CHURCH

(1567–1622)

He was born in Savoy to an ancient and noble family. He studied law at the universities of Paris and Padua, but in the end, he chose an ecclesiastical life. Right away he was appointed provost of the cathedral of Geneva, but this was only an honorary title, as there was no way for him to get into this city so firmly in the hands of Calvin's followers.

Getting Geneva back was the burning question of the day for the Catholics of Savoy, and almost everyone was thinking in terms of an armed conflict, according to the custom of the time.

Francis decided, instead, "to knock down its walls with charity, to invade it with charity, to reconquer it with charity". He himself became a missionary and preacher, encroaching on Calvinist territory, even though he knew each time he was risking his life. His preaching was never violent, but always persuasive and convincing.

He even invented the system of pamphleteering, having affixed to the walls or slid under the doors of houses slips of paper he himself had prepared with brief summaries of Catholic doctrine (this would gain for him the title of patron of journalists).

Elected bishop of Annecy-Geneva, he exercised broad pastoral action at the European level, but afterward chose a modest way of life, preferring to dedicate himself personally to the ministry of confession and to the education of children.

Together with Saint Jane Frances Frémiot de Chantal, he founded the institute of the Visitandines. During the last years of his life, he composed two spiritual works that gained him the title of Doctor of the Church: the *Introduction to the Devout Life* and the *Treatise On the Love of God*, in order to spread and illustrate the teaching that holiness is possible for every Christian in every state of life.

He left an indelible memory of his meekness and his great pastoral charity and died as a venerable man who had always remained a child in the hands of God. It was the feast of the Holy Innocents in 1622.

Saint Alphonsus Maria de Liguori
BISHOP AND DOCTOR OF THE CHURCH
(1696–1787)

He was born in a suburb of Naples and was very young (just sixteen) when he earned the title of doctor in jurisprudence. In his exercise of the legal profession, he won great fame for his expertise and honesty, but he was upset when he lost cases on account of cheap legal chicanery. So he decided to leave the profession in order to dedicate himself to works of mercy.

One day in a hospital ward, he felt in his heart the invitation of Jesus, saying to him, "Leave everything and dedicate yourself only to Me." He chose the way of the priesthood and dedicated himself to preaching in poor neighborhoods and in the countryside, gathering around him a great number of coworkers, including laity.

In 1732, he founded the Congregation of the Most Holy Redeemer, the members of which (who are called Redemptorists) took particularly to heart the evangelization of the most isolated rural areas, using a simple style of preaching in contrast with the affectation customary at the time.

In 1762, although he was already seriously ill, he had to accept the episcopacy. But he lived another twenty-five years, dedicating himself to the care of the diocese and to studies in moral theology, of which he became an undisputed master for the whole Church, able to combine firmness and meekness. And so he has continued down to our own day.

He also published countless spiritual works intended for ordinary Christians. The two most famous ones are entitled *The Glories of Mary* and *The Practice of Loving Jesus Christ*.

Alphonsus was also a skilled musician, and some of the traditional melodies most loved by the people are his, like the famous Italian Christmas song "Tu scendi dalle stelle".

He lived to a very advanced age and, during his last years, was not even capable of celebrating Holy Mass, but spent hours and hours in front of the tabernacle and the rest of the day reciting ejaculatory prayers every now and then.

On July 29, 1787, he said:

"Give me Our Lady."

He clasped in his hands the image they gave him, and his death agony began. He was gasping, but at times he would smile at the image, and it seemed he was speaking with her under his breath.

He lasted this way for two more long days. On the first of August, 1787, as the midday Angelus bell was ringing, he expired. All the days of his life, from childhood to old age, Alphonsus had always wanted to kneel down at the sound of the bells that commemorated the Incarnation, even if he was on the public roadway. And as an old man, afflicted as he was with arthritis, he crumpled to the ground each time without being able to get up on his own.

But that last day, the ones who came to lift him back up were the angels.

Saint John Vianney

PATRON OF ALL PARISH PRIESTS

(1786–1859)

He was called Jean-Baptiste-Marie Vianney and had been born in France during the revolutionary tempest. Because of this, he had received his First Communion in hiding, in a barn fitted out as a church.

With no standard education, he made it through to ordination with the help of an old parish priest. At the age of thirty-two, he was appointed curate for Ars, a small and almost completely dechristianized parish, rich only in taverns and dance halls, where the good curate began to do himself what almost no one did any more: he spent long hours in church adoring the Most Holy Sacrament and praying for his parishioners, doing penance for their sins.

Partly out of curiosity and partly out of the need for a good word or two, people started coming back to the parish church little by little, and crowds began to form outside the confessional, where sinners learned repentance by kneeling in front of that strange priest who spoke about the mercy of God with tears in his eyes.

After ten years, the parish of Ars had become known all over France. Endless streams of pilgrims poured in, obliging the holy curate to stay in the confessional from dawn until late at night, no matter what season of the year. He had to elbow his way out in order to celebrate Holy Mass and provide a little catechism for his parishioners, in a tone that was always humble but forthright.

The years went by, and the elderly curate continued to feel unworthy of being pastor, to ask forgiveness, and to forgive, while his parishioners were already selling his image to pilgrims as that of a saint. He had become an old man of seventy-three with long white hair, a diaphanous and worn-out body, and eyes that were ever more profound and luminous.

In that blistering hot summer of 1859, his parishioners, gathered around the poor rectory, had even covered the whole building with ten drop-cloths that they wetted periodically so he would not have to suffer too much from the oppressive heat, at least in those last days.

On August 4, he died without agony, without fear, "like a lamp that has run out of oil, having in his eyes an extraordinary expression of faith and happiness".

Then, for ten days and ten nights, his mortal remains had to remain on display in that chapel where he had heard so many confessions, while pilgrims filed past uninterruptedly by the thousands.

In one of his most beautiful prayers, the holy curate had already described how he would like to die: "I love You, O my God, and my only desire is to love You until the last breath of my life. I love You, O my infinitely lovable God, and I would rather die loving You rather than live without loving You. I love You, Lord, and the only grace I ask is to love You eternally [. . .] My God, if my tongue cannot say in every moment that I love You, I want my heart to repeat it to You as often as I draw breath."

Saint John Bosco
EDUCATOR AND FOUNDER
(1815–1888)

Born in Castelnuovo d'Asti to a family of farmhands, John lost his father at the age of two and was brought up by his mother, Margherita, who would always remain his most faithful coworker. Physically gifted, as a boy he entertained his peers in order to lead them to Christian instruction.

He became a priest in 1841, when the city of Turin was at a fever pitch of industrialization and was bringing in swarms of young people who were often exposed to vice and crime. For their sake, Don Bosco founded an Oratory, open to all youths no matter what their origin or capabilities.

A born educator, he was a convinced proponent of the "preventive method", which consists in "knowing how to get everything from the students with love and not with force", accompanying them in such a way as to "make up for their shortcomings in advance".

After various attempts, the Oratory was established in Valdocco. The boys were provided with housing and with training for the most varied trades. In 1862, it already numbered more than seven hundred boys. With a first nucleus of confreres, in 1854, Don Bosco set up the Society of Saint Francis de Sales (later called the Salesians). To this was added later the Pious Union of Salesian Cooperators and the Daughters of Mary Help of Christians.

Less remembered today but of incalculable importance was his activity also as a writer and publisher, which the saint developed—always with the intention of educating young people—notably ahead of his time.

When he died, his initiative already numbered sixty-four houses in twelve countries and more than a thousand religious.

In the days of his death agony, at times while dozing he would relive his old worries over his boys. One day he awoke with an anguished cry: "Hurry, hurry quick to save those young people! Mary Most Holy, help them. Mother, Mother!"

They suggested he ask Mary Help of Christians for the miracle of healing, but he refused and said only: "Lord, may your will be done. O Mother, Mother, open for me the gates of heaven."

What he had in his heart as he was dying we know from what he had repeatedly said to his boys: "I have promised to God that until my last breath I would be for you young people. I study for you, work for you, am even willing to give my life for you. Realize that what I am, I am all for you, day and night, morning and evening, at every moment." And to one of his close associates, during those last days, he urged:

"Tell the young people I am waiting for all of them in heaven."

Saint Daniele Comboni
MISSIONARY AND FOUNDER
(1831–1881)

He was born in Limone sul Garda, the only survivor of eight children. Educated at the Collegio Don Mazza in Verona— an environment particularly sensitive to the missionary issue —Daniele decided to consecrate himself forever to Africa.

He departed for the Sudan in 1857, with several companions who, however, died almost right away: in those years, European missionaries could not withstand the African climate.

Back in Italy, in 1864, Comboni composed a brilliant "Plan for the Rebirth of Africa", to suggest a new missionary method aimed at "saving Africa with Africa". The plan was to have European missionaries open schools on the African coast (where the climate was bearable even for them), in which they would form African priests, sisters, doctors, and teachers. It would then be these who would penetrate the interior of the continent and take the lead in evangelization. Comboni traveled all over Europe to discuss his plan with the most important missionary organizations of the time, but he did not succeed in getting any concrete support.

So he decided to do it on his own: in 1867, he founded the Comboni Missionaries of the Heart of Jesus and in Cairo opened the first schools to prepare the future African evangelizers.

In 1870, in Rome, although he was just an ordinary priest, he was given permission to explain his plan to the Fathers of Vatican Council I, securing the approval of Pius IX, who in 1872 appointed him Apostolic Provicar for central Africa.

Right away, Daniele also founded the women's institute of the Pious Mothers of Nigritia. Consecrated bishop in 1877, he fought hard against the pashas and governors who were allied with the slave traders, to defend his beloved black faithful.

A few years later, the "holy war" broke out, declared by the Mahdi, a self-proclaimed prophet who said he had been sent by God to free the Sudan from the Turks and from Christian influence.

Comboni immediately got news of the first skirmishes and of the first massacres of government troops. He wrote about these to his friends in Italy, concluding with a mixture of anguish and Christian hope: "Cheerful! We will go to heaven sooner. Viva Gesù! I find myself here on the battlefield exposed to losing my life at any moment for the sake of Jesus and for the infidels, while I am oppressed and immersed in an ocean of tribulations that are tearing my soul apart."

He died two months later, at the age of just fifty, struck down by cholera. Shortly afterward, the Mahdi would destroy all of his work and even his tomb, and they would keep his surviving missionaries prisoner for seventeen years.

But Comboni—who had lived "in the heart of Africa and with Africa in his heart"—had died with the certainty that "his work—born at the foot of the Cross—would not die."

Saint Leopold Mandić
CONFESSOR
(1866–1942)

He was born in Herceg Novi (then in Dalmatia, today part of Montenegro). Physically frail, small of stature, and of humble appearance, he was accepted at the age of sixteen into the Capuchin seminary of Udine, and here he began to work on his character, which was rather touchy and impetuous, and to live a very intense life of faith, centered above all on the Eucharist.

After becoming a priest, he made the resolution of dedicating his life to the reconciliation of the Orthodox Slavs with Rome. He wanted to go to the East, but in 1906 he was sent to Padua, which would become his adoptive and definitive homeland, on account of the great and tireless apostolate that he would carry out there, above all as a confessor.

So the little friar became convinced that the Lord was binding him to the city of Saint Anthony: "My East is here!" he told himself, making a vow to welcome with all care any penitent who came to him from then on.

When he was not in prayer, he was in the confessional, spending from ten to fifteen hours a day there, literally besieged by penitents, who found in him the sweetness and at the same time the firmness of Jesus.

"How do you manage to stand it for so long?" one of the other friars asked him.

"It is my life, you know?" Father Leopold replied with a smile, remembering the vow he had made.

Ever more slight in body, with his hands deformed by arthritis, a stutterer with bloodshot eyes, he exercised a powerful attraction for anyone who was seeking the mercy of God. He was a living exemplification of the merciful father of the Gospel parable.

Given his naturally fiery character, he felt close to those who were fragile. Until old age, he strove tirelessly with an extraordinarily serene spirit, determined to "die of apostolic toil", as he had taught the younger friars.

His greatest sufferings—which stayed with him even on his deathbed—were due to the fact that he had spontaneously offered himself to God in expiation for the sins of his penitents. This meant that Father Leopold was burdened with the anguish of those he had comforted and to whom he had said, "I will do penance myself!"

This is why none other than he—who had generously administered God's mercy to all—sometimes spent nights consumed with the fear of divine justice. His attendant said he seemed like Jesus on the Cross, when he was weighed down by all the sin of the world and felt abandoned by the heavenly Father.

But the end came with sweetness, even though a terrible illness (a tumor of the esophagus) had been destroying him for some time.

That last morning of his life, July 30, 1942, he fainted after getting ready to celebrate Mass. He came to again on his cot and humbly received the last sacraments. Then, while he was reciting the *Salve Regina* with the other friars, at the words "O clement, O loving, O sweet Virgin Mary", he drifted off, like an elderly child in the arms of the one he had always tenderly called (in the old Venetian language) *la Paròna benedeta.*

Saint John XXIII

POPE

(1881–1963)

Born in Sotto il Monte (Bergamo) to a farming family of simple and generous faith, Angelo Roncalli was still a child when he chose the path of the priesthood. Ordained a priest at the age of twenty-three, he ran the gamut of ecclesiastical careers, becoming first a seminary professor and then secretary of the bishop of Bergamo. During the First World War, he became a military chaplain. After the war, he founded and ran the Student House in Bergamo and was assistant of the Young Women of Catholic Action, in addition to being a spiritual director at the seminary. In 1921, he was called to Rome as coordinator of all the missionary activities of all the Italian dioceses. At the age of forty-four, he was appointed apostolic visitor for Bulgaria and was consecrated bishop. After ten years, he was appointed apostolic delegate for Turkey and Greece and apostolic vicar of Constantinople. He also gained the respect and trust of the Orthodox and Muslims. In 1944, he was sent to France as apostolic nuncio. In 1953, he was appointed cardinal and patriarch of Venice.

On October 28, 1958, he was elected pope and took the name of John XXIII. Three months after his election, he was already announcing his intention of convening an ecumenical council so the Church could rephrase for the modern world—with new language and missionary passion—

the ancient truths of the Christian faith. To the Church and humanity, he gave two beautiful and decisive encyclical letters in particular: *Mater et Magistra* and *Pacem in terris*.

His last public appearance took place on the feast of the Ascension in 1963. On that occasion, almost as a farewell and a final encouragement, he said, "Let us run behind the Divine Teacher who goes up . . ."

On May 30, he received the last sacraments, and those present heard his parting words:

"This bed is an altar; the altar needs a victim: here I am, ready. I offer my life for the Church, the continuation of the Ecumenical Council, the peace in the world, and Christian unity. Many have asked me about the secret of my priesthood. . . . Well then, today I believe I can give the answer. The secret of my priesthood lies in the crucifix that you see before me, in front of my bed. He looks at me, and I talk with him."

And after a pause, almost as if summing up his life, "I have had the supreme grace of being born in a modest and poor but God-fearing Christian family, and of being called to the priesthood. Ever since I was a child I thought of nothing else, I desired nothing else. My earthly day is ending, but Christ lives, the Church goes on."

His death agony would last for three more days. He died on June 3, 1963, in the late afternoon. And the last words he spoke to his secretary were these: "Why weep? This is a moment of joy, a moment of glory."

Meanwhile, in Saint Peter's Square—filled with a silent and emotional crowd—a Holy Mass was celebrated for the dying pontiff, who expired as the celebrant pronounced the concluding words: *Ite missa est*, as if to confirm that John XXIII, priest of God, had fulfilled his long ministry.

Blessed Charles de Foucauld
"UNIVERSAL BROTHER"
(1858–1916)

He was born in Strasbourg and lived a wayward youth, "denying nothing and believing in nothing", devoting himself only to cultivating his pleasures. He undertook a military career but was dishonorably discharged "for breach of discipline aggravated by bad conduct". He then dedicated himself to travel, exploring an unknown area of Morocco, an enterprise that earned him a gold medal from the Geographical Society of Paris. He returned to his country shaken by the all-encompassing faith of some of the Muslims he had come to know in Africa. He came back to Christianity and converted radically, making his first confession ever.

Determined to "live only for God", he joined the Trappist monks at first but left after a few years to go to the Holy Land and live there like Jesus, in poverty and obscurity. Ordained a priest for the sake of being able to celebrate and adore the Eucharist in the most remote areas of the world, he returned to Africa.

He established himself near an oasis deep in the Sahara, wearing a simple white robe on which he had sewn a red heart with a cross on top. To Christians, Muslims, Jews, and idolaters who came by his oasis, he introduced himself as "universal brother" and offered hospitality to all. Afterward, he pushed even farther into the desert, reaching the Tuareg village of Tamanrasset.

He spent thirteen years there, occupying himself with prayer (to which he dedicated eleven hours a day) and with composing an enormous French-Tuareg dictionary (still used today) as a tool for future evangelization.

But first he had completed the text most decisive for them, noting: "I have just finished the translation of the Gospels in the Tuareg language. It is a great consolation for me that their first book should be the Gospels."

On the evening of December 1, 1916, his home—always open to visitors—was raided by a gang of bandits.

The two thousand pages of the French-Tuareg dictionary were strewn around the floor and trampled. Father Charles was tied up with camel reins, probably to be taken as a hostage, but was killed in a moment of panic with a rifle shot to the head.

His end was unexpected, but not a complete surprise. In one of his notebooks, these words had been traced and re-traced boldly, almost as if for a memento: "To live today / as if I were to die / this evening / a MARTYR."

No one worried much about the death of that strange hermit. Amid the ongoing military clashes, it was considered just one more episode, not worthy of special attention. The French commander of Fort Motylinski let three weeks go by before carrying out an inspection in Tamanrasset.

When he got there, he found almost buried in the dust the monstrance that still contained the consecrated Host. From heaven, perhaps Father Charles' heart went out to Jesus-as-Eucharist, who had remained completely alone for so long in the desert.

For his beloved Tuareg (who had become his brothers, even though they were not yet baptized), he had kept to the end the Word of God, embodied in the Gospels and in the Eucharist.

Saint Pio of Pietrelcina
THE PRIEST WITH THE STIGMATA
(1887–1968)

Francesco Forgione had become a Capuchin at the age of fifteen and had taken the name of Pio. Ordained a priest in 1910, he had been sent to San Giovanni Rotondo, a town in the Gargano. He would stay there for more than fifty years, marked by the grace of the stigmata he received in 1918 (which he called "my crucifixion"), immediately the object of admiration for many and of calumny for some.

Floods of pilgrims started to pour into San Giovanni Rotondo, and the first miracles and sensational conversions began to take place. There were two overwhelming experiences that left their mark: the Holy Mass, which Padre Pio celebrated as if he were reliving the events of Calvary and the sacrament of confession he administered, in which many sinners vividly perceived the embrace of divine mercy.

Padre Pio was confrontational and curmudgeonly with penitents who were motivated by empty curiosity or the intention to justify themselves, but he became meek and sweet as could be when he saw signs of true repentance.

On account of the spread of silly or pointless popular accounts and demonstrations of mindless fanaticism, Padre Pio was placed under investigation by the Holy Office, which imposed painful restrictions that he accepted in humility and obedience, without ever playing the victim.

He said all he cared about was "having God always fixed in the heart and stamped on the mind". Concerned about the overall well-being of his children, he also brought about the creation of the *Casa Sollievo della Sofferenza* (Home for the Relief of Suffering), a hospital that was to be supported by prayer groups spread all over the world.

During the night between September 22 and 23 of 1968 (he had just commemorated the fiftieth anniversary of the day on which he received the stigmata), after making his confession and renewing his religious profession, Padre Pio, crumpled in his armchair and dressed in his beloved habit, died clasping in his fingers the beads of the rosary and murmuring: "Jesus . . . Mary".

When they arranged his dead body, the friars realized the five wounds—which had bled for fifty years and during those last days had begun to close over—were not there; not even a trace of scarring could be seen in their place: The flesh was intact and soft and seemed—so to speak—resurrected.

He died at the age of eighty-one, and it seems more than a hundred thousand persons took part in his funeral.

"Father," his devotees had asked him, "how will we get by when you are not here anymore?"

He had replied: "Go before the tabernacle. In Jesus, you will also find me."

Saint Josemaría Escrivá

FOUNDER

(1902–1975)

He was born in Barbastro, in northern Spain, and became a priest at the age of twenty-three. From the time of his adolescence, he predicted that God wanted to entrust to him a special mission, which was made clear to him in October of 1928: to promote, among persons of every social class, the search for holiness and the exercise of the apostolate through the sanctification of work.

He dedicated himself to gathering a few laypeople around him in order to propose holiness to them as a vocation that was possible even in the world and in the exercise of their profession. This was the birth of Opus Dei.

During the Spanish Civil War (1936–1939), Josemaría was forced into exile and was not able to return to Madrid until after the conflict was over. The Opus then received a new impulse, and its members were motivated to live in the world, whether in positions of responsibility or in humble occupations, with the conviction that nothing can hinder the holiness of a layman if the environment in which he is called to live is conceived of and approached as a "vocational setting".

Escrivá's constant teaching was that "the Cross must also be inserted in the very heart of the world. Jesus wants to be raised on high—there: in the noise of the factories and workshops, in the silence of libraries, in the loud clamor of the streets, in the stillness of the fields, in the intimacy of the family, in crowded gatherings, in stadiums. . . . Wherever there is a Christian striving to lead an honorable life, he should, with his love, set up the Cross of Christ, who attracts all things to himself."[4]

On February 14, 1943, he also founded the Priestly Society of the Holy Cross. He went on many trips all over the world, to spread everywhere the vision of "a world christianized by the laity".

Among all of these, one particularly moving and prescient one was a trip-pilgrimage to the shrine of Guadalupe, in Mexico. He was enchanted and remained gazing for hours at the image of the Virgin offering a rose to the Indio Juan

---

[4] Josemaría Escrivá, *The Way of the Cross* (New York: Scepter, 1983), chap. XI, Points for Meditation, no. 3.

Diego, and he said with shining eyes, like a dreamy child: "It would be so beautiful to die like that, in front of the Virgin, who is offering you a rose!"

On March 28, 1975, he celebrated the golden anniversary of his priesthood. He said: "Fifty years have gone by [after my ordination] and I am still like a faltering child. I am just beginning, beginning again, as I do each day in my interior life. And it will be so to the end of my days: always beginning again."

He had exactly three months of life left. On June 26 of that same year, while returning to his office, he suddenly collapsed to the floor, right in front of a reproduction of Our Lady of Guadalupe.

And he died as he had wished, having before his eyes the image of the Virgin offering a flower to her humble devotee.

CHAPTER VII

Dying Innocent

From the first centuries, the Church has placed in her liturgical calendar, the feast of the Holy Innocents as a permanent reminder that holiness (including that of those who give their lives for Christ) is, in the first place, a gift. But she has also done so in order to recall that this "holy belonging" to the Lord Jesus can be given to us from the tenderest age. It is always remembered that the children of Bethlehem died as infants: they could not even talk yet, but they bore witness with their whole little selves.

And they died innocent: they were no harm to anyone, but already evil flooded over them "like a furious storm over rosebuds", as an ancient Latin hymn says.

Their whole ordeal shows us, in essence, Jesus when he was not yet two years old, protected and proclaimed by this band of little martyrs who hide and shelter him from the wrath of Herod.

In continuing and developing this first Christianized "icon", we could recount today as well the innocent death (which is always a true martyrdom) of so many children who are mistreated and destroyed in body and soul.

We would like, instead, to recount the nonviolent death, but marked by awareness of the Gospel, of a few young people and children who accepted with holy Christian maturity a death that others would have called premature and therefore unjust, while they embraced it, for Jesus' sake, with sincere and fervent love.

A death that—in God's plan—did not take place by an oversight of his Providence, but in order to call the Church and all mankind to rethink "the school of life".

It is lovely, in this regard, to recall and suggest the reading of *The Mystery of the Holy Innocents*, written by Charles Péguy in 1912.

> You send children to school, God says.
> I think it is to forget the little they know.
> It would be better to send the parents to school.
> It is they who have need of it.
> But naturally it would have to be a school of mine,
> And not a school of men.
> You believe that children know nothing.
> And that parents and grown-up people know something.
> And it is the children who know Everything.
> For they know first innocence.
> Which is everything.
> Life also is a school, they say. You learn something every
>   day.
> I know that life which begins at Baptism and ends at
>   Extreme Unction.
> It is a perpetual wearing away, a continual spreading decay.
> One is always going downwards. . . .
> They cram themselves full of experience, they say; they
>   gain experience; they learn about life; from day to day
>   they accumulate experience. A singular treasure, God says.
> Treasure of emptiness and want. . . .
> Treasure of wrinkles and anxieties. . . .
> As for what you call experience, your experience, I call it
>   waste, diminution, decrease, the loss of innocence.
> And a perpetual degradation.
> For it is innocence which is full and experience which is
>   empty.

It is innocence which wins and experience which loses.
It is innocence which is young and experience which is
  old. . . .
It is innocence which knows and experience which does
  not know.
It is the child who is full and the man who is empty.[1]

So let us begin with a saint who is little known but enchanting through her powerful innocence.

Saint Rose of Viterbo
(1233–1251)

The Gospel says the kingdom of heaven is for those who
"become like children". This indication is usually taken at
the personal level as an invitation to spiritual childhood,
characterized by simplicity, trust in God, and abandonment
into his paternal hands.

But there are, in the history of the Church, eras and situations so hardened and degraded that God chooses actual
innocent creatures to speak to the mighty and powerful who
wage war at the expense of poor Christians.

Such was the era in which Rose of Viterbo lived, when
Frederick II was fighting against Pope Innocent IV and
the people were ferociously divided into Ghibellines and
Guelphs. What importance and power could ever be wielded
by a girl of modest circumstances, not yet fifteen years old,
who went around the streets of the city poorly dressed and
with a little cross in her hand, preaching peace in the name
of Jesus? And yet the powerful of the time went so far as
to exile her under the accusation that she was "inflaming

---

[1] Cf. Charles Péguy, *The Mystery of the Holy Innocents and Other Poems*,
trans. Pansy Pakenham (New York: Harper, 1956), pp. 134–37.

spirits". But it was only the fire of innocence that made evident the malice of the strong and the sorrow of the humble.

Apart from this, there is not much information about this young saint, who had been gravely ill since birth and yet courageous and indomitable. She died in part on account of the cold she endured when, in order to make her be quiet, her family was exiled to a town in the mountains.

Even her miracles are tender, like that of the hunks of bread she hid in her apron to give to the poor.

"What are you hiding?" snapped her father, who was rather stingy.

And the girl, frightened, replied, "Roses."

And roses were all her stubborn father found when he investigated.

There is a similar episode in the life of Saint Elizabeth of Hungary. She was a queen; Rose, however, was so poor that not even the poor nuns of San Damiano had wanted to accept her into their monastery. And she had quipped in reply: "You do not want me alive, but you will be happy to have me when I am dead."

And this is what happened when, after she was proclaimed a saint, the people of Viterbo chose her as their patron.

During a pastoral visit, Saint John Paul II said to them: "What a great response of love we find in that marvelous young woman who was your Saint Rose! She, in spite of the changing times, still presents herself today as a model for girls and young women, inviting them to understand through and through, in their lives, the absoluteness of God in a full donation of love beyond all human respect!"

Saint Kateri Tekakwitha
(1656–1680)

She was canonized in 2012: the first Native American saint, a member of the Mohawk Nation. She was born in 1656 in the Mohawk village of Ossernenon to an Iroquois father, who was a pagan, and an Algonquin mother, who was already a Christian. She lost her parents at the age of four, during a smallpox epidemic that also left her face disfigured and her eyesight weakened. Brought up by an anti-Christian uncle, she preserved in her soul the memory of the hymns and prayers that she had heard her mother sing that enchanted her and she repeated during her long walks through the forests. She was seeking and loving Someone she did not know but whose presence she intuited to the point of offering Him her spousal love (in a sort of impromptu consecration).

At the age of twenty, a Jesuit missionary baptized her. Opposed by relatives on account of her new faith and harassed by bothersome suitors, she fled on foot, covering almost two hundred miles until she reached the Catholic mission du Sault Saint Louis, near Montreal.

So on Christmas of 1677, she was able to receive her First Communion and finally satisfy that "unquenchable thirst for spiritual things" which she had always felt. At the feast of the Annunciation, the following year, she renewed with full awareness her old virginal consecration. What little strength she had left was employed in giving assistance to children, the elderly, and the sick.

She died at the age of twenty-four, and right away the scars left by the smallpox disappeared from her face, as if Jesus had given her His first caress, leaving her face luminous. She is invoked as the Lily of the Mohawks and has been given the title patroness of the environment and ecology.

Saint Dominic Savio
(1842–1857)

In him, Don Bosco saw realized, as if by a miracle, what he wanted for all the boys of his Oratory. He was a sweet and well-mannered child, already in love with holiness. When they met for the first time, Don Bosco (referring to Dominic's mother's job as a seamstress) said to him, "It seems to me that there is good fabric in you. . . . We can make a beautiful garment to give to the Lord."

And the boy agreed joyfully.

That the fabric was truly exquisite was something Don Bosco's mother, Margherita, also understood right away, saying to her son, "You have many good young people, but no one surpasses the beautiful heart and the beautiful soul of Dominic."

The holy educator was so convinced of this, he often asked for his help in showing the ropes to the more unruly and rebellious boys.

"We here", Dominic explained to them, "make holiness consist in staying very cheerful. Let us seek only to avoid sin, because it is a great enemy that steals from us the grace of God and our peace of heart."

He also founded, with a few friends, a Company of the Immaculate Conception in order to provide help for their more disadvantaged companions, in doing homework or at play.

Unfortunately, the boy's health was very fragile, and the

doctor advised that he take a break from his studies and go back to his hometown, thinking the familiar atmosphere and his mother's care could do him some good.

Dominic could find no peace over this. On the last evening of his stay at the Oratory, the boy peppered Don Bosco with questions, "What is the best thing a sick person can do to please the Lord? From heaven will I be able to see my companions of the Oratory and my parents? Will I be able to come visit my friends?"

"He seemed", Don Bosco wrote, "like a person who already had one foot in heaven and before entering it wanted to be well informed on the things he would find there."

At home, he had to undergo the treatment, in vogue at the time, of repeated bloodlettings, and the boy readied himself for the sacrifice by thinking "of the nails planted in the hands and feet of Our Lord". After a few days of useless and torturous treatment, the boy was completely exhausted, although he still found the strength to recite, at the crucifix on the wall of his room, a little poem he had always loved: "Lord, all my freedom I give to you. / Here are my powers, my body! / I give it all to you, which is all yours, O God, / And to your will I abandon myself."

When the moment arrived, Dominic himself said to his father: "The hour has come. Get my book of prayers, and read me the prayers for a good death."

And to the traditional invocations he responded with infinite devotion: "Merciful Jesus, have pity on me."

When the prayer came to the words "My God, receive me into the loving bosom of your mercy", he sighed: "That is just what I want!"

He died in his parents' arms, saying to his mother, "Mother, don't cry, I'm going to heaven."

And to his father: "The most beautiful thing I have ever seen!"

To Don Bosco—appearing in a dream—he explained, "It was Mary Most Holy who came to get me: my greatest consolation in life and in death. Tell her children never to forget to pray to her."

Saint Maria Goretti
(1890–1902)

She was born in Corinaldo, the third daughter of two poor farmers who had moved to an old farmhouse. Little Maria had not been able to study: all she could manage to do was to prepare for her First Communion, but she had matured in the sweetness of the faith, which she learned from the lips of her parents, reciting prayers with them in the morning and the rosary in the evening. She was responsible for the housework and the care of her younger sister.

Her father died when Maria was only ten years old, and her mother had to set up house with another family of farmers. One of the members was Alessandro, a restless twenty-year-old who began to take an unwholesome interest in the little Maria, who was not yet twelve years old.

One hot day in July of 1902, seeing the girl was alone in the house, Alessandro tried to use violence on her. Maria reacted by making a powerful appeal to his Christian faith.

"It is sin, Alessandro. You will go to hell!" she repeated, trying to break free.

Exasperated, the young man pounced on her with an awl, stabbing her a number of times.

Drawn by the shouts, her relatives came running, and four hours later the nurses with a horse-drawn ambulance came for her. At the hospital of Nettuno, the doctors realized nothing could be done about Maria's fourteen wounds, although she was still conscious.

Before she died, she said to the priest who was tending to her, "I forgive Alessandro with all my heart, and I want him to be near me in heaven."

The young man was incarcerated, but one night he dreamed Maria was gently inviting him to a life of repentance and faith. He converted in prison, where he remained for twenty-seven years. And he was present at Saint Peter's on June 24, 1950, the day of the glorious canonization of his victim.

Blessed Laura Vicuña
(1891–1904)

She was born in Santiago, Chile, but her family—in the wake of political upheavals—had been forced to take refuge in a miserable village on the border with Argentina. Her father died of privation, and her mother, in order to survive, accepted the attentions of a rich and violent cattle rancher.

Fortunately, during those very years the first Salesian missionary sisters arrived, and the girl was enrolled in their little school. With the sisters, Laura was happy, although in her heart she concealed a growing suffering on account of her mother's humiliation, of which she was gradually becoming more aware.

The situation became intolerable during vacation time, when the man tried to abuse her as well.

So the little girl started to anticipate anxiously the day of her First Communion: she had decided to consecrate herself to Jesus and to settle the painful question with him directly. She could not forget the terrible night when the rancher had whipped her mother before her eyes because she would not let him abuse her daughter.

After she received First Communion at the age of ten, Laura became more joyful and more mature. On the night of July 16, 1903, the school was hit with a terrible flood. On account of the cold she suffered and the continual persecutions of the rancher, Laura's health declined rapidly.

Forced to move back in with her mother, she suffered new attacks by her persecutor, resisting courageously. Then, in spite of the fact that she was feverish, she ran away to take refuge once again in her little school, where she arrived in a state of exhaustion.

She received extreme unction on January 22, 1904, the feast of Saint Agnes, and on the occasion asked her confessor for permission to tell her secret to her mother, "Mother," she said to her, "I am dying. I myself asked Jesus for this. . . . For two years now I have offered my life to Jesus for you, so that you would return to him. Won't you give me this joy before I die?"

The woman, meanwhile, had knelt down weeping next to her child's bed. The revelation had wounded her to the depths of her soul. But perhaps she had already guessed it some time before. She had only the strength to say to her: "I swear to you that I will do what you ask me. . . . I am repentant, and God is witness of my promise."

At the sound of the evening Angelus bell of that same day, Laura, knowing she had fulfilled her mission, after kissing the crucifix again and again, expired as she was still saying, "Thank you Jesus; thank you Mary! Now I die content."

Her classmates came running. The people of the town came running. And all were saying to each other: "The little saint has died!"

At the funeral, everyone saw her mother, repentant and

trembling, receive the sacraments, and they understood. And those who knew all the ordeals the little one had gone through invoked "Laura, virgin and martyr", while her mother—remembering what her daughter had had to endure—agreed amid her tears, "Yes, virgin. And martyr for me!"

Blessed Francisco Marto
(1908–1919)

He is one of the Little Shepherds of Fatima: he was just nine years old at the time of the apparitions, when Our Lady had asked: "Do you want to offer to God an act of reparation for the sins by which He is offended and for the conversion of sinners?"

Francisco had agreed passionately. All the more so in that Our Lady had promised to take him to heaven soon. But she had urged him to recite many rosaries first.

"O my Lady! I will say as many rosaries as you wish!" the child had replied.

But there was one detail that filled him with anguish, and he often pointed it out to Lucia, "Haven't you noticed that Our Lady was so sad when she asked that sinners stop offending God, who is already so greatly offended? I would like so much to console Our Lord."

This became his interior passion. He often repeated, "But how awful that He should be so sad! If only I could console Him!"

And so, when visitors and investigators became bothersome to him over the question of the apparitions, Francisco would say to Lucia: "Let it go! Didn't Our Lady say that we would have to suffer much in reparation to Our Lord and to her Immaculate Heart for the many sins by which they are offended? They are so sad! If we can console them with these sufferings, we should be happy!"

He was the first to fall ill during the 1919 Spanish flu epidemic that decimated Europe. But he bore everything without complaining, because he wanted to go through with his task all the way to the very end. He was very quiet; he would speak at length only with Lucia or with his little sister.

"Go to church," he said to his cousin, "and keep the hidden Jesus company for me. What makes me suffer the most is that I can no longer go to spend a little time with the hidden Jesus."

Lucia often urged him, "In heaven do not forget to pray for sinners, for the pope, and for me . . ."

"Listen," Francisco replied, "ask Jacinta for these things. I am afraid I will forget them when I see Our Lord, and besides, most of all I want to console Him."

Before he died, he repeated to Lucia: "It's not long now before I'll be going to heaven. Up there I will console Our Lord and Our Lady very much. Meanwhile, Jacinta will pray very much for sinners, for the Holy Father, and for you, and you will stay down here because Our Lady wants it. Listen, do everything she tells you!"

He expired on April 4, 1919—less than two years after the apparitions—exclaiming, "Mother, look over there by the door, what a beautiful light."

He was just eleven years old.[2]

---

[2] Francisco Marto, beatified on May 13, 2000, was subsequently recognized as a saint and canonized on May 13, 2017.—ED.

Blessed Jacinta Marto
(1910–1920)

She was two years younger than Francisco, but she survived him by one year.[3] She got sick together with her brother, but her illness was longer and more painful.

She, too, tried never to complain and to offer everything, "I suffer all for the conversion of sinners and in reparation for offenses against the Immaculate Heart of Mary", she said to Lucia.

And she added, "I don't want anyone to know about my sacrifices, because they belong only to Jesus and Mary."

One day she said to her, "I can no longer get out of bed and prostrate myself on the floor, or I will fall. I must content myself with kneeling."

To the very end, she had tried to prostrate herself in order to do as the angel had taught her. She calmed down only when they explained her prayers were pleasing to the Lord even if she was lying down. But still she was gripped by the desire to have something to offer.

"Tonight I was in great pain, and I wanted to offer Our Lord the sacrifice of not turning in bed."

She was always absorbed in prayer. She said, "I think of Our Lord, of Our Lady, of sinners, of the war that must come. . . . There will be so many homes destroyed, so many priests dead. . . . How awful!"

To Lucia she confided everything, "I love the Immaculate Heart of Mary so much. It is the heart of our Heavenly Mother! Doesn't it please you immensely to repeat many

---

[3] Like her brother, Francisco, Jacinta Marto was subsequently recognized as a saint and canonized on May 13, 2017.—ED.

times: Sweet Heart of Mary, Immaculate Heart of Mary? I like it so much, so much."

And when she found out her cousin had just received Communion, she begged her, "Come here, right beside me, while you have in your heart the hidden Jesus." They gave her an image of the Sacred Heart.

"How ugly it is!" she said, thinking about the beautiful face she had contemplated.

Then she gave in: she brought the image to her lips and said, "I will kiss it on the heart, which is the part I like best!"

She was the youngest: she loved much, and much was asked of her.

One day, from her bed, she asked to have Lucia come quickly and told her, "Our Lady came to see me; she says that she will come very soon to take Francisco to heaven, and she asked me if I still wanted to convert more sinners. I answered yes. She told me that I will go to a hospital and there I will suffer much. . . . I asked her if you were coming with me. She said no. This is the hardest thing for me. She said that Mother will take me to the hospital, but then I will be left there alone!"

She remained silent, suffering visibly, then she added, "If only you were coming with me! . . . What is hardest for me is going there without you! Perhaps the hospital is a very dark house where you can't see a thing, and I will be there suffering all alone! But it doesn't matter, I will suffer out of love for the Lord, in reparation to the Immaculate Heart of Mary, for the conversion of sinners, and for the Holy Father."

And she prepared to face that solitude which frightened her.

When Francisco was about to die, Jacinta sent him this

message: "Give many greetings to the Lord and to Our Lady. Tell them that I will suffer all they wish for the conversion of sinners."

Her Calvary began: they took her to a first hospital where she stayed for two months, coming out in worse condition than when she had gone in. Then an illustrious physician came to Fatima and convinced her parents to send the child to Lisbon, to undergo a difficult surgical operation. She left in tears.

"I'm going to die alone!" she said repeatedly.

Lucia tried to comfort her, "Don't think about it!"

And she replied, "I have to think about it. . . . I want to suffer for the love of Jesus and of sinners."

She kissed the crucifix and repeated to Him, "Jesus, I love you, and I want to suffer much for your love. Now you can convert many sinners, because this sacrifice is very great."

They had promised her she would be staying with a rich family, but when the rich family saw the condition of the sick girl, they refused to take her. She ended up in an orphanage, happy because it was "the house of Our Lady of Fatima". And the superior of the orphanage truly acted as a mother for her, giving her all the tenderness the little girl needed.

On top of this, Jacinta was happy because she could receive "the hidden Jesus" every day. From Lisbon, she sent word to Lucia that Our Lady was coming to visit her often. The superior recounted, in fact, that one day she had gone to visit the little girl, who was lying in bed, but Jacinta had said to her, "Come back later, little mother, because now I am waiting for Our Lady."

But she had to leave even this last refuge when they moved her to the hospital for the surgical operation that had to be done under only partial anesthesia—on account of the patient's extreme weakness—and was extremely painful. At one point, when she just could not take it anymore, she suddenly became peaceful. She said, "Our Lady came to visit me, and she took away the pain."

Ten days after the operation—which according to the doctors had been a complete success—she expired, attended only by the nurse. She was just ten years old.

"What I felt close to her", Lucia later testified, "was what one feels close to a holy person who seems to communicate with God in everything."

Venerable Antonietta Meo
(1930–1937)

The holiness of such a little girl as this was certainly a gift of God, but also a wonder of her upbringing. At the age of five and a half, she was diagnosed with a sarcoma on her knee, and her leg had to be amputated. A year later, the cancer came back and metastasized, leaving her just three months of life, in unspeakable suffering.

But the experience of Nennolina (as she was called in her family) was not only painful, it was extraordinary, because she was helped to treasure her suffering as one treasures a precious gem in order to offer it to the beloved. She lived her suffering in the company of Jesus. Even more (although this may seem incredible to us): she lived it in the company of the Most Holy Trinity.

Remembering the sufferings of Jesus was not an expedient dreamed up by adults in order to convince a poor little girl to accept her cruel suffering, but it was a reality that was good, loving, profound, a substance that was mysterious yet real, redemptive, that she had learned to love from her earliest years. And many Christian parents know with what tenderness and realism children are often able to look at the image of the Crucified, with a desire to console Him in His pains.

In the family, everyone helped each other to live that domestic drama: Nennolina, Father, Mother, her older sister, the maid, even the doctors, one of whom, an atheist, converted at that incredible spectacle.

Decisive were the days of preparation for First Communion, which Nennolina was able to receive at the age of six.

Around seven in the evening, when the prosthesis became unbearable, Nennolina had to go to bed, and her mother spent a great deal of time with her. First, they said prayers together, then her mother recounted something from the Gospel, and finally the little girl wrote a letter to God and left it under a statuette of the Child Jesus: the one that depicts Him sleeping on a cross that serves as his crib. Between October 15th and Christmas of 1936, she composed 106 of these, dictating them to her mother.

With touching spontaneity, the child became ever more familiar with the world of God-as-Trinity: at times, she addressed her little letters to "dear Jesus"; at times, she addressed herself to "dear God the Father"; and at times, to "dear Holy Spirit". In many instances, she would ask One to share with the Other her questions or her endearments.

Nennolina took an interest herself in everything, interceded for everyone, talked with them about everything, with astonishing maturity.

She died at the age of seven, after undergoing a final and extremely painful surgical operation.

She had asked, "Mother, how does one manage to die?"

And her mother responded with incredible power and beauty: "I commended my heart to the Lord that He might inspire me and transform my words into truth, and I replied, 'One feels a great desire to die, and the soul flies into the arms of Jesus.'"

The little girl smiled, but she explained that she did not want to rest in heaven, but to go to work for the conversion of souls, like Saint Thérèse of the Child Jesus. The saint of Lisieux had brought upon the earth a shower of roses. She, Nennolina, smaller and white, promised to make it rain lilies.

While she was preparing to receive daily Communion, held up in the bed by her parents, she gasped, "God! Mother! Father!"

And she expired. Meanwhile, the priest was coming in through the door with the Eucharist. Her mother and father received it for her.

Venerable Maria del Carmen González-Valerio

(1930–1939)

She was born in Spain, during the years in which a civil war had erupted that left hundreds of thousands of dead on the battlefield, accompanied by an anti-Christian persecution with thousands of martyrs. Given the circumstances, she received First Communion when she was not yet six years old, and her prayer was that of the little Thérèse of Lisieux which she had been taught: "O my Jesus, I am all yours. You have given yourself to me, and I give myself entirely to You."

Before two months had gone by, her father was taken by communist militiamen.

"Do not cry, I am dying for God and for them", Don Julio said to his wife, indicating the children. "One day, when they are grown up, you will explain to them how I died. I am dying so that the holy crucifix may return to the classrooms to protect the childhood of our children, and so that they may be brought up in a Catholic Spain."

Right away he was barbarically murdered. From that day, the whole family knew they were in danger, the children already marked down on a list of those to be deported to Russia. Instead, they made their getaway to France.

Maria Carmen's decisive maturation took place at the age of nine, during the ceremony of Holy Thursday, when the little one unexpectedly asked her grandmother for permission to *entregarse* ("offer herself"), asking also for a detailed explanation of the meaning of that action about which she had heard.

"It means to give oneself entirely to God and be all God's", her grandmother told her.

And the girl lived that act as the offering of her very life. Shortly afterward, she came down with scarlet fever, with painful complications and sufferings she bore without complaint, as if she had a mission to fulfill.

This would become clear later, when (after her death) they would find in her handbag a diary bundled up and secured with adhesive paper, on which it was written: "Private, private, private", as children do when they don't want anyone to read their secrets.

Three of the pages are important. On the first, she noted: "August 29, 1938. Today they killed my father." On one of the last pages she wrote: "Viva España. Viva Cristo Rey!" (the dying cry of the martyrs who were being killed for their faith). But on the front page of the diary is written: "I offered myself at the Parish of the Good Shepherd, April 6, 1939."

The family doctor testified: "The child gave transcendence to her suffering. . . . This was what for me, as a doctor, caused true astonishment. The love inside this child was so extraordinary that it impregnated her whole little body, and in every look, in every gesture, in every attitude, one noted a profound mystical love that the little one treasured in her heart."

She kept with her a little book of prayers entitled *My Jesus,* and in her better moments she read the reflections presented there.

But the nurse noticed the little one almost always put the bookmark on a page dedicated to death: on it was a picture of an angel holding a child in his arms. She only took care to make sure her mother did not notice.

And the reflection that Maria Carmen read often was this one, "When one hears singing from a bush, it is not the bush that is singing but some little bird that is hidden in there. We too think, love, remember things. . . . But the one who thinks, loves, remembers is the soul. And the soul is spirit and will never die."

On the morning of July 17, 1939, she said, "Today I am going to heaven."

Then she wept and asked forgiveness of her nurse because, she said, she had not loved her very much, and to all her relatives present she repeated, "Love one another."

Then she said, "Let me, let me go."

"Where do you want to go, little one?" asked her grandmother.

And the answer was, "To heaven, Grandmother, don't you see that the Virgin has already come to get me?"

Blessed Chiara Luce Badano
(1971–1990)

She was born in Savona, but spent her childhood in Sassello, a charming little Ligurian town between the Apennines and the sea, in a good and solid Christian family. Her father was a truck driver (rather serious and demanding); her mother a factory worker (particularly sweet and attentive), and both of them showered her with care and affection after spending the first eleven years of their marriage sighing and praying for a child.

Her good family upbringing was brought to completion when the girl was able to participate at the age of nine (she was in third grade) in a meeting of Gen 3, the "New Youth" of the Focolare movement.

She thus learned to live with *Jesus in the midst*, diving into activities of unity and charity, and spent a cheerful and lively adolescence: loving music, sports, friendship, literature, the sea, the mountains.

Her meeting with Chiara Lubich, the founder of the movement, was decisive, and the young woman wrote to her: "Dearest mother, during this congress I have rediscovered the Gospel in a new light. I have understood that I was not an authentic Christian, because I was not living it through and through. Now I want to make this magnificent book the only aim of my life. I do not want to and I cannot remain illiterate with respect to such an extraordinary message. Just as easy as it was for me to learn the alphabet, so it should also be to live the Gospel."

At the age of sixteen, she went through a crisis, probably occasioned by the move from one group to another, as is customary in the movement as one gets older, and by the changes in her peer group and responsibilities. She stayed away from some of the meetings and ran the risk of breaking off the journey that had helped her so much. "The ideal was in danger of being put on the back burner", she would later recount. But then she got back into it, agreeing to become the leader of a group of younger girls. So she resolved her initial crisis by deciding to make the girls entrusted to her happy, dedicating herself to "cementing their unity" with a thousand agreeable inventions dictated by friendship and faith.

The drama began in the summer of 1988 with severe pain in her shoulder during a tennis match: at first they thought she had cracked a rib; then they resorted to infiltration, until she was finally given a CAT scan and was diagnosed with bone cancer. This began a continual *via crucis* around the various hospitals of Turin, until February of 1989, when Chiara underwent her first serious surgical operation. When she came out of the anesthesia, she was heard to murmur, "Why, Jesus?"

And immediately afterward, "If you want it, I want it too!"

But the medical report (stage four osteosarcoma, the most serious form, with metastasis from the beginning) left no hope of recovery.

It could have been the hour of darkness, but from the spirituality of the Focolare movement, Chiara had long since learned *love for the abandoned Jesus.*

In the hospital, she also had the chance to talk with a nurse who was going through a crisis and refused to accept "that God who permits the suffering of children". We do not know what Chiara said to her, but the nurse would later tell everyone it was the most beautiful Christmas of her life. On the ward, everyone was amazed by the luminous intensity of her gaze.

Meanwhile, she was comforted by the correspondence she carried on with Chiara Lubich, to whom she wrote: "I would be happy if you could choose my new name (if you think it is appropriate)", receiving this reply: "Chiara Luce is the name I have chosen for you. It is the light of the Ideal that overcomes the world."

So the young woman was able to leave this life happy

in bearing that new name which is also the legacy that she wanted to leave to the world: Chiara Luce Badano, a genuine program of the heart, of the soul, and of the eyes, become a gift for all. (Another gift was that of her corneas—the only part that had remained untouched—which she decided to donate upon her death). Meanwhile, with her closest friend, who almost never left her side, Chiara played "God's game": she knew Jesus was about to arrive and decided to prepare herself as a bride prepares. She got a white dress, very simple but elegant; she sent her parents to buy nice new clothes —as is fitting for a daughter's wedding—she selected the songs and rehearsed them with her friend. Everything was to be joyful. To her mother she said, "When you are dressing me, you must not weep, but say: now Chiara Luce is not suffering anymore, she sees Jesus! When I come into church you must sing, because I will be singing with you."

She wanted everyone to be in harmony with heaven.

"When an eighteen-year-old girl comes to heaven, they celebrate!"

She died on the feast of Our Lady of the Rosary, stroking her mother's hair and saying to her, "Bye-bye, be happy, because I am."

"She was able to turn her passion into a wedding song", Chiara Lubich wrote of her afterward.

One day, almost lost in thought, the young woman had said to her mother, "Who knows who will come to meet me when I get to heaven?"

And her mother said right away, "The first will certainly be Our Lady!"

And Chiara said, "Hush! Don't ruin the surprise for me!"

All young saints have suffered, not because suffering is necessary for young people to be holy but for the simple fact of the brief span in which they have completed their existence, cut off by illness or violence. But suffering is not the point of view from which to judge their holiness; it is, instead, the miracle of a love that attains its fullness in a brief time and in dramatic situations.

A young person who suffers always attains an objective sacredness, but his holiness then depends on the dialogue that he is able to maintain with Christ, in joy and in pain.

If it is true that we are all called to holiness, it follows from this that God is close in a special way to all suffering young people and offers them particular graces for the realization of such a holy project.

Many times the ultimate outcome of this *getting close to God and with God* remains hidden or is shown only in fleeting glimpses, because of the profile of the sufferer and the countless and various influences of relatives, teachers, friends, doctors, etc.

But when a special holy radiance is produced (as in the cases of the holy young people and children we have recalled here), then there is wisdom in attentively studying how the pedagogy of God and that of men have been interwoven. We can say that in holy young people—in the brief years of their earthly lives—there takes place the fascinating adventure of a youth that does not wither, not even when the body shows its decay. And it is a miracle of communion, in which the grace of God and the humble good will of the creature work together, without always being able to distinguish the divine action from the human, because both are substantiated by a love that becomes ever more *one*.

Moreover, the lives of young saints certainly display a unique divine pedagogy: with them and for them God has had to "hurry up" in His love: He has had to be very rich in gifts, and the creature has had to be very generous in response.

But for us, there remains the task of studying them closely, of understanding why and how the pedagogy of God has been able to assert itself and obtain the results desired by heaven.

CHAPTER VIII

Dying as Saints

Under this heading we would now like to recall the lay saints distinguished only by having been ordinary Christians whose vocation situated them *in the world*. They are called, by virtue of their baptism, to become saints in the sacred spaces of everyday life, "in a special way [making] the Church present and operative in those places and circumstances where only through them can it become the salt of the earth" (*Lumen Gentium*, no. 33).

If, therefore, every believer learns to offer his entire existence to the Holy Spirit of Christ, the baptized layman offers it to Him precisely where His thoroughly incarnated existence is rooted in the world: he shapes it and is shaped by it. At his disposal, for the sake of this task, he has none other than "the energy [that] is a gift of the Creator and a blessing of the Redeemer" (ibid.), an energy both created and restored, natural and supernaturalized.

Family and work are the "places of the world" in which lay Christians participate in the affairs of all men, dealing with the same worldly material but handling it in an ecclesial manner. They call "love" the work that is due to persons, and they call "work" the love that is due to things, but all is for building up their own family and the human family.

This is how they become priests for the world, by devoting themselves to consecrating it to God, in its very *material*, human and earthly, "making Eucharist of all things". *This* is how they proclaim Christ in the common conditions of the world: little by little as the Word becomes life in their lives, and little by little as their whole existence resounds as a word of salvation right in the middle of the world's commotion. And above all, they proclaim it from one generation to the next, the most essential transmission, communicating it with their lives to their own children. *This* is how they allow Christ to reign, honoring Him well in the service they render freely in all settings, whose reality is a gift from God that is waiting to be wisely developed for His glory.

By belonging to the Lord Jesus and building up His Church in the world, the laity are "simply Christians", and by fulfilling their mission with joyful obedience, they can become "simply saints". This does not change the fact that their existence must often reach peaks of true and heroic fidelity. But the word *saints* has the same sound it had at the beginning of Christian experience, when the word served to indicate all the baptized "called to be saints" (1 Cor 1:2).[1]

Blessed Elisabetta Canori Mora
(1774–1825)

Elisabetta Canori belonged to a prosperous Roman family. At the age of twenty-two, she married the young lawyer Cristoforo Mora, but the happiness of the two young people was soon destroyed by the psychological and emotional fragility of her husband. Won over by the enticements of a woman of low station, he stayed out until all hours of the night, squandering the family's inheritance and reducing it to poverty.

[1] Cf. Acts 9:13; 1 Cor 16:12, 15; 2 Cor 8:4.

Drawing strength from intense prayer and from the conviction that the sacrament of matrimony had truly bound them together in a precious and indissoluble way, Elisabetta resolved on total fidelity to her husband and their two daughters, whom she supported laboriously by her own work. She honored the sacrament she had received, although she was forced to do so alone, venturing onto a "mystical" terrain made of inexhaustible charity, aid for other families in difficulty, the attentive upbringing of her daughters, and getting to know Jesus her Bridegroom, who assisted her with miracles of love.

Her husband—who could find no peace in the faithfulness and honor he knew he did not deserve but received nonetheless—outwardly displayed scorn toward so much humble dedication, but on the inside he was shaken by his wife's holiness. After she died, in fact, Cristoforo converted to the point of becoming a Conventual Franciscan friar and priest.

At the end of her life, Elisabetta said to her confessor, "At times I am sweetly penetrated by the spirit of the Lord, as if immersed in a vast ocean. I find myself filled with grace, overcome with love; my heart expands, and I make it as big as I can, while I would like to love my God as much as all of heaven loves Him."

More than a year in advance, she predicted the exact day of her death, in addition to which God had given her a foretaste of it, moment by moment, in a vision she recounted, "It seemed to me that I was expiring in the arms of Jesus and Mary, enjoying a paradise of satisfaction."

As the fateful day drew near, she told her daughters, "I leave you, as a Father, Jesus the Nazarene."

And she urged them always to respect and help their father.

Saint John Paul II beatified her in 1994, calling her *a woman of heroic love.*

Venerable Margherita Occhiena
MOTHER OF SAINT JOHN BOSCO
(1788–1856)

She was an illiterate young farm worker, but she showed herself to be a wife and mother of rare perfection, with innate gifts as an educator. She attentively followed her son's vocation, instilling her immense faith in him and watching from a distance, amazed, the work he did, constantly surrounded by hordes of young people in need of everything. When Margherita reached the age of fifty-eight (a somewhat advanced age for the time), Father John—finding himself in a particularly dire situation—asked his mother to come live with him and help him in his mission.

"If you think this will please God, I am ready to leave right away."

She sold a piece of her farmland in order to have a bit of ready money and brought along with her the trousseau she had succeeded in keeping intact during those difficult years. She set out for Turin on foot and was exhausted by the time she got to the apartment that had already been rented in the Pinardi house in Valdocco, on the outskirts of Turin: one room for Margherita and one for Father John, a kitchen and a guest room. Behind the house was a shed that would serve as a chapel for the young people. The oratory was supplied by a vast meadow nearby, and it was there that more than two hundred young people welcomed Don Bosco, who had come back along with his mother. She began her work by making a few liturgical vestments for her son from the bridal gown she had jealously preserved. The rest of her trousseau she adapted for use as household linen. Her wedding ring and bridal necklace went toward the first payment on the rent. Mother Margherita ran an ironing and mending workshop, where she was assisted by a few coworkers, and looked after the big room where the community's clothing and linen were kept.

When her strength gave out, she was forced to stay in bed, and her room became a pilgrimage destination for young people, who looked in asking for news about her health; most of the visits were paid by those who were with Don Bosco as his seminarians and disciples, intent on continuing his work. When it was time for her to receive viaticum, Margherita struggled to speak to her son, "When you were a child, I helped you to receive the sacraments. Now it is your turn to help your mother: I am unable to say the words clearly; you say them out loud, and I will repeat them in my heart."

Then, although she had always been shy about using expressions of affection, she added, "God knows how much I have loved you, how much more I will love you from heaven."

From her son her thoughts went naturally to those countless children mired in suffering outside her door, "Tell our dear little children that I have worked for them, and that I love them like a mother. Have them pray for me and make at least one *Communion* for my soul."

She died at three in the morning on November 25, 1856, at the age of sixty-eight. From the day of her marriage, she had lived all of those years, right to the last hour, as a mother.

Blessed Frédéric Ozanam
(1813–1853)

He was born in Milan in 1813, to French parents. He spent
his childhood and youth in Lyon, a city in the grip of the
industrial fever, where the dramas of the society and Church
of the time were more clearly perceptible. He was diligent
and successful in his studies and at the age of eighteen moved
to Paris to enroll in the Faculty of Law and Letters at the
Sorbonne. Out of 2700 students, only a dozen or so were
openly Christian. So Frédéric began to rebut, with detailed
written and oral arguments, the anti-Christian accusations
and insinuations that professors were spreading in the class-
room, also organizing together with his friends conferences
on history and philosophy.

Immersed in that fierce cultural battle, there was only one
objection that touched him deeply, that of those who asked,
"Tell us what you are doing, you Catholic students, for the
poor!" From that moment on, the invitation Frédéric issued
to his friends was, "Let's go to the poor!" This led, with the
same missionary impulse, to the creation of the Society of
Saint Vincent de Paul, so that faith and charity, culture and
social action could develop in harmony. At the beginning,
there were only eight students, who in eight years grew to
two thousand in Paris alone. After twenty years, there were
more than five hundred Societies of Saint Vincent all over
France.

Meanwhile, Ozanam had become one of the youngest and
most esteemed university professors and was given the post
of Foreign Literature at the Sorbonne. Studying the differ-

ent forms of literature and their origin, Ozanam responded effectively and in detail to the thesis in vogue at the time that saw Christianity as the cause of the decline of the ancient Roman, French, and Germanic civilizations. In his lectures, he demonstrated, to the contrary, the fruitfulness of their encounter with Christianity. He even found that this shed light on the difficult situation of the Church in his time, which also had to learn to "go over to the barbarians". It was an appeal addressed to the Church—for centuries allied with the nobility and middle class—to ally itself finally "with the people who have too many needs and not enough rights". This was, according to Ozanam, the true Christian response to the continual insurrections of the poor and the working class that were afflicting France during those years. After marrying Amélie Soulacroix and becoming the father of a little girl, Frédéric lived conjugal and family life in the fullest awareness of the sacrament on which all of it was founded, thus realizing in this field as well a complete identity as a Christian layman, intent on rooting the Gospel in the temporal world.

The world in which he lived his vocation as a husband and father is witnessed to by a tender gesture he performed on the last anniversary of his marriage (fifteen days before he died, at the age of forty!): walking along a beach in Antignano, he saw a myrtle branch in bloom, which in antiquity was a symbol of love and beauty. He had it picked and gave it to his wife with a poem he had written:

> You, my guardian angel, remain here below,
> but it will be your prayer that opens heaven for me.
> You remain yet awhile to be with the girl,
> the tender child who is the cause of our joy.

Have her think of me, but give her your virtues.
We will meet again where love is forever
and exchange before the very eyes of God
the long embrace that will never end.

He died after renewing, together with his wife, their wedding vows. To those who asked him if he were not afraid of meeting God, he replied, "Why should I be afraid of him? I love him!"

Saint Zélie Guérin
(1831–1877)

and

Saint Louis Martin
(1823–1894)

They are the parents of Saint Thérèse of Lisieux, who left us this testimony: "God gave me a father and a mother more worthy of heaven than of earth."[2] "I have had the good fortune to belong to Parents without equal."[3] "It was [God] who had her born in a holy soil."[4]

They had nine children, four of whom died young, and this is how Zélie remembered the years spent having and raising them: "We lived only for them. They were all our happiness, and we never found any except in them. In short, nothing was too difficult, and the world was no longer a bur-

---

[2] Letter from Thérèse to l'abbé Bellière (LT 261) in *Letters of St. Thérèse of Lisieux*, trans. John Clarke, O.C.D., vol. 2 (Washington, D.C.: Institute of Carmelite Studies, 1988), p. 1165.

[3] St. Thérèse of Lisieux, *Story of a Soul*, trans. John Clarke, O.C.D., 3rd ed. (Washington, D.C.: ICS Publications, 1996), p. 16.

[4] Ibid., p. 15.

den to us. For me, our children were a great compensation, so I wanted to have a lot of them in order to raise them for Heaven."[5]

The pregnancies were often difficult. "At times, M. Martin himself worried." The mother reassured, "Do not fear; God is with us."[6]

Thérèse was able to get to know her mother only during the first four years of her life, but she noted: "God granted me the favor of opening my intelligence at an early age. . . . Jesus in His love willed, perhaps, that I know the matchless Mother He had given me, but whom His hand hastened to crown in heaven."[7]

And what she remembered most was how right away she considered her mother's arms a "heavenly enclosure", and how she learned to pray from her: "I loved God very much and offered my heart to Him very often, making use of the little formula Mother had taught me."[8] To the point that the little girl understood her mother was dead the morning on which—taken to the home of friends—she realized no one was concerned about having her say her prayers.

Zélie died prematurely of a tumor, amid unspeakable suffering that she accepted with complete and saintly resignation. At the end of the tragic last December of her life, she was able to affirm, "I am like children who don't worry about tomorrow, I am always waiting for happiness."

[5] Quoted in the epigraph to Fr. Stéphane-Joseph Piat, O.F.M., *A Family of Saints: The Martins of Lisieux—Saints Thérèse, Louis, and Zélie*, trans. by a Benedictine of Stanbrook Abbey (San Francisco: Ignatius Press, 2016), p. [5].

[6] Ibid., p. 116.

[7] Thérèse of Lisieux, *Story of a Soul*, p. 17.

[8] Ibid., p. 38.

This is how one of her daughters described her last days:

> When she grows tired of supporting her head, we very gently lift her up together with the pillows so that she is sitting up completely. But it's never without incredible pain because at the least movement she lets out harrowing cries.
>
> And yet how patiently and resignedly she bears this dreadful illness. She never puts down her rosary; she still prays despite her suffering, we all admire her for it, for nothing can match her strength and energy.
>
> A fortnight ago she was still saying the whole rosary on her knees at the foot of the Bl. Virgin in my bedroom that she loves so much. Seeing her so sick I wanted to make her sit down, but it was pointless.

She died at dawn on August 28, 1877. The last lines she scribbled were: "If the Blessed Mother [of Lourdes, where she had gone on pilgrimage] doesn't cure me, it's because my time is at an end, and God wants me to rest elsewhere other than on earth."[9]

Louis Martin, her beloved husband, survived her by seventeen years, taking care of their daughters with such tenderness that Thérèse considered him an earthly image of "Papa the good God". The years spent with him are recounted, in the autobiography she wrote, with the embellishment of a thousand little annotations like this: "[I had] only to look at him to see how the saints pray"; "When I think of you, little Father, I naturally think of God, for it seems to me that it is impossible to see anyone more holy than you on the earth."[10]

---

[9] Piat, *Family of Saints*, p. 221.

[10] Thérèse of Lisieux, Letter to M. Martin, July 31, 1888 (LT 58), in *General Correspondence*, vol. 1, trans. John Clarke, O.C.D. (Washington, D.C.: Institute of Carmelite Studies, 1982), p. 452.

Her father's illness coincided with the first years of Thérèse's monastic life as a Carmelite, and she learned, looking at him, how one manages to remain always a child of God, like Jesus disfigured by suffering.

During the last meeting she had with her ailing father, at the monastery grate, when his daughters were saying "see you later", Louis could only laboriously raise his eyes and point upward with his finger. He stayed like this for a while, then struggled to utter, "In heaven!"

In the hospital where he stayed, they attended to him as one attends to a saint. He still had good moments, and everyone saw that the bent of his heart and mind was unchanged.

"Ask Saint Joseph that I may die as a saint", he whispered one day to the daughter who was looking after him.

He died at the age of seventy-one, his eyes fixed on the daughter beside him, who was reciting the beautiful prayer that begins: "Jesus, Joseph, and Mary, I give you my heart, my life, and my soul."

A few years before, Thérèse had written prophetically: "Soon we shall be in our native land, soon the joys of our childhood, the Sunday evenings, the intimate chats . . . all this will be restored to us forever and with interest. Jesus will return to us the joys He has deprived us of for one moment! . . . Then from our dear Father's radiant head, we shall see rays of light coming forth, and each one of his white hairs will be like a sun that will give us joy and happiness!"[11]

---

[11] Letter from Thérèse of Lisieux to Céline, July 23, 1891 (LT 130), in *Letters of St. Thérèse*, 2:732.

Blessed Giuseppe Tovini
LAWYER
(1841–1897)

Born in the province of Brescia during the second half of the nineteenth century, he found himself living in an age in which "the upper hand had been gained by ideologies hostile to the Catholic tradition of the country."

He specialized in jurisprudence and exercised the legal profession with "uncommon juridical and rhetorical expertise", practicing his craft with true missionary passion. A friend was able to say of him: "He never worked just for money, but he worked quite a bit for the poor."

One could say that, without ever neglecting the family and professional duties that were already piling up for him —but reducing them to the essential, on account of the urgency of the times—he dedicated all his remaining resources of energy, intelligence, and heart to the mission of making the faith present and active in society.

In his view, his main task was to instill a Christian presence in the schools (which he called "our Indies") and in education. Evening classes, circulating libraries, reading and recreation groups, scholarships, academic clubs, initiatives for the preservation of faith in the schools, dormitories, the league of Catholic teachers (for pension and insurance purposes) were just a few of his projects. He became one of the directors of the *Opera dei Congressi* and was the first Catholic elected to the city council of Brescia, which at the time was in the hands of the liberal and secularist left. But he was also active in the domains of journalism, the banks, labor groups, and universities. He participated in the foundation of numerous rural credit unions, the Banca San Paolo in Brescia, and the Banco Ambrosiano in Milan. In 1888, he founded the Initiative for the Preservation of the Faith in the Schools in Italy, which by 1891 was already producing the magazine *Fede e Scuola*. In 1893, he created the League of Catholic Teachers and the magazine *Scuola Italiana Moderna*, the first national pedagogical and didactic periodical.

A husband and the father of ten children (whom he taught that "in order to do some good, one must strive to do something great"), he always considered "the Church as his family and his family as the Church". While his overwhelming activity was still in full swing, his always precarious health finally failed him. His lungs were infected with tuberculosis, and he was almost constantly feverish, but the fever that tormented him seemed almost the expression of an even more ardent interior fever that was consuming him. The continual travels—often in bad weather—continual conferences, continual speeches, continual vigils brought home just how worn out his body was. Exhausted, at the age of fifty-five he died. That last afternoon, his wife had to take from his hands the paperwork he had been asked to complete on behalf of a religious institute.

"You are my paradise", Giuseppe said to her during those days, looking at her with the same affection as always.

And his wife, as a good Christian, became a bit worried, thinking she was almost a distraction for him in that solemn hour. But Tovini had considered the whole Church as his family, working to safeguard her and to earn for her (yes, for the Church!) even material bread and all necessary goods. And that last gaze of the dying man, grateful for the tenderness of his wife, understood by that time the reality beneath the veil of the sacrament.

Saint Giuseppe Moscati
PHYSICIAN
(1880–1927)

Born in Benevento, in 1897 he enrolled in the faculty of medicine of the University of Naples, deliberately confronting the positivist and practically atheist environment and coming out unscathed and, on the contrary, in love with his faith and his virginal dedication to Christ the Lord.

After graduating with honors in 1903, he chose the Hospital of the Incurables, where he got to know better the meaning to be given to the exercise of his profession, understood as a tireless service-apostolate but also as the duty to cultivate fully his own scientific preparation while at the same time cultivating the closest unity between science and faith, between professionalism and charity, also expressing this unity in the comprehensive attention he wanted to devote to his patients. In emergency situations (first with the 1906 eruption of Vesuvius and, a few years later, with the cholera epidemic), he was able to lavish his efforts to the limits of exhaustion, drawing his strength both from his medical passion and from the Eucharist he received every day. In 1911, he was made a university professor and also produced numerous scientific essays that brought him worldwide fame. He never stopped making house calls and dedicated himself above all to the sick poor, from whom he did not accept any payment; instead, he himself paid for the medicines he prescribed. He had set for himself as his ideal *to love God, without measure in love, without measure in suffering.* The target of vulgar attacks by his Masonic and anti-clerical colleagues, who set out to destroy and annihilate him, he never concealed his faith.

We know almost nothing about his death, because it came about through a sudden illness. But he was in the habit of talking about it as if he had a date with it. To those who asked him if he were afraid of death, he replied, "So far I do not have this fear, and I hope, with God's help, never to have it."

He also added, "For those who are prepared, a sudden death is best."

So he died at the age of forty-six, and even his adversaries finally paid him the honor due to his intelligence and his charity. While the funeral procession was winding through the streets of Naples, with an immense throng of professors, students, and ordinary people, a little old man approached the table that had been set up in the foyer of the Moscati home and in the registry of condolences wrote with a trembling hand: "We weep for him because the world has lost a saint, Naples an exemplar of every virtue, and the sick poor have lost everything." He was canonized by Saint John Paul II in 1987, at the end of the Synod of Bishops on the *Vocation and Mission of the Laity in the Church and in the World*.

Servant of God Madeleine Delbrêl
SOCIAL WORKER
(1904–1964)

By the age of seventeen, she was already a staunch atheist. The problem of faith came up, but not because she was looking for comfort. She wrote: "A hundred worlds even more desperate than the one in which I lived would not have made me waver if they had proposed faith to me as a consolation."

What made her waver was instead an unexpected occur-
rence:

> Meeting a number of Christians no older, no more stupid,
> no more idealistic than I, who lived the same life as I did,
> discussed as much as I did, danced as much as I did. On
> the contrary, they had some advantages on their side: they
> worked more than I did, had academic and practical train-
> ing that I did not, had political convictions that I did not.
> They talked about everything, but also about God, who
> seemed as indispensable to them as air. They were at ease
> with everyone, but—with an impertinence for which they
> sometimes even apologized—they brought into all of their
> discussions, plans, memories, words, ideas, the finishing
> touch of Jesus Christ. They could not have made Christ
> seem more alive if they had brought Him in and had Him
> sit down.

No longer sure about the nonexistence of God, she decided she had to start praying, and the miracle happened.
Later she would use the term "bedazzlement" and would
say: "Then, reading and reflecting, I found God; but in
praying, *I believed that God had found me* and that He is the
living truth that can be loved as one loves a person." She
thought about becoming a Carmelite, but since her family
situation would not permit it, she decided to live as a contemplative in the world. She had this one plan clearly in
view: "Voluntarily to belong to God as much as a human
creature can wish to belong to the one he loves. To be voluntarily the property of God, in the same total and exclu-
sive manner, definitive, public, in which a religious becomes
so in consecrating herself to God." In order to remain in
close contact with the poor and the working classes, she
chose to become a social worker. Together with three companions, she moved to Ivry (a town near Paris), opening
a Center of Social Action. In 1938, Madeline gave them

a mission statement: *We, people of the street,* a proclamation affirming that there are Christians for whom "the street"—meaning the spot in the world in which God puts them—is "the place of holiness", as the monastery is for consecrated persons.

So for a long time, she lived in "Marxist territory", carefully distinguishing between the persons God entrusted to her and their ideology, without ever being afraid to get involved in a just cause.

She already felt weary at the age of just sixty, but she continued to find the thought of death extremely repugnant. She said, feeling a bit guilty, "Probably I was baptized only halfway."

But she consoled herself with the thought that "Jesus also felt a sort of indignation every time He found Himself in the presence of death."

Yet her capacity for loving identification with others was intact. A photo from July of 1964 (three months before her death) shows her curled up on the floor in front of a little girl, and between them is a spinning top.

On October 13, 1964, in Rome—for the first time in the history of the Church—a layman spoke in the council hall, addressing all the bishops of the world on the theme of the apostolate of the laity.

On that same afternoon, in Ivry, Madeleine collapsed at her desk. She had taken leave without disturbing anyone. . . . In her missal, her companions found a few words dating back to ten years earlier, which she had written to commemorate the thirtieth anniversary of her conversion. To mark her radical abandonment to God that had ripened over those years, she had written:

> I want what you want
> without asking myself whether I have the capacity

without asking myself whether I have the desire
without asking myself whether I want it.[12]

Servant of God Giorgio La Pira
MAYOR OF FLORENCE
(1904–1977)

Born in the province of Ragusa, after a very wayward youth
he returned to God following an encounter with a cultured
and holy priest who opened wide for him the world of faith
and prayer, getting him to see that life was made "for building a thousand bridges between earth and heaven" and that
the mind and heart of man were "windows open on the
supernatural world".

He moved to Florence to study Roman law and at the age
of thirty was already a university professor.

Elected a member of the Constituent Assembly of the
Italian Republic, he went on to become a member of parlia-
ment and minister of labor. In 1951, he was elected mayor
of Florence, his adopted city, which he administered over
multiple terms on the basis of this political principle: "In every city worthy of this name, everyone must have a home
for loving, a school for learning, an office for working, a
hospital for healing, a church for praying. And then many
gardens, so that children may play and the elderly may rest
in holy peace."

Particularly close to his heart was the role of Florence in
the world. Florence was for him the city of beauty, where
the Christian faith and humanism had kissed forever. Florence was the city of dreams that embodied the dream of
all cities. And La Pira decided to call to it representatives

---

[12] Madeleine Delbrêl, *The Joy of Believing*, trans. Ralph Wright (Sherbrooke, Que.: Éd. Paulines, 1993), p. 21.

of all the peoples on a pilgrimage of friendship, peace, and culture. He began to organize Conferences for Peace and Christian Civilization every year, inviting for dialogue men of culture from every background (there were also Arabs, Jews, Africans . . .), on issues that he himself selected and introduced.

The first conference was entitled "Civilization and Peace". This was followed in subsequent years by "Prayer and Poetry, Culture and Revelation", "Theological Hope and Human Hopes", "History and Prophecy", with an ever-growing number of participants. These were the postwar years in which nations were still closed in on themselves, and dialogue was almost nonexistent. La Pira had restored the Salone dei Cinquecento in the Palazzo Vecchio and had made it sparkle with beauty: here he welcomed his guests, put them at their ease, listened to them, and asked them questions, proud of that "Council of Nations" which was not yet universal but already significant.

He suffered, however, because it was not yet possible to get representatives from Eastern Europe across the Iron Curtain. So he invented, in 1955, the Conference of mayors of all capitals of the world, and this was the first time the mayor of Moscow and the mayor of Beijing came to the West. This allowed him to establish relations no one else had been granted to that point, even traveling to Russia in 1959 as the first Western politician invited to speak at the Kremlin.

In spite of the immense credit La Pira had gained throughout the world, he spent the last ten years of his life forgotten and overlooked by everyone, seen as an idealist and a dreamer. The only one who was there to comfort and reassure him was an elderly priest (Father Facibeni, known in Florence for his immense charity, whom everyone called "the Padre"), who with great gentleness reminded him of the most consoling truth: "God never abandons us. He is with us: in our hands, in our eyes. When God seems to abandon us, it is because He wants to accomplish with us a work that is greater than ourselves."

He received the most beautiful recognition after his death, when his casket was carried by the workers of a foundry whose jobs La Pira had guaranteed by fighting with them and for them. He has been called "the saint of Christian hope".

Saint Gianna Beretta Molla
PEDIATRICIAN AND MOTHER
(1922–1962)

She was born in Magenta, in the province of Milan, to a family with solid Christian roots. She decided to study medicine, specializing in pediatrics, in part because she dreamed of going to join her brother, a doctor who had become a Capuchin missionary in Brazil. Instead, she met and married the engineer Pietro Molla, wanting to live her marriage as an incarnation of God's infinite love for His creatures.

Their home was gladdened by the birth of three children. In the summer of 1961, Gianna immediately welcomed another pregnancy with joy, even though there was no lack of concern over a fibroma that was growing next to the uterus. Repeatedly advised to resort to abortion, Gianna absolutely refused, agreeing with her husband on the decision to save the baby first.

The girl was born beautiful and healthy, but Gianna died a few days later, happy with her sacrifice and her obedience to God. The deeper explanation for such a dramatic decision was given by her husband:

She did not do what she did "to go to heaven". She did it because she felt like a mother. In order to understand her decision, one cannot forget, in the first place, her profound persuasion as a mother and as a doctor that the creature she bore within herself was a complete creature, with the same rights as other children, even though she had been conceived just two months before. A gift of God deserving sacred respect. One also cannot forget the great love she had for her children: she loved them more than she loved herself. And one cannot forget her trust in Providence. She was convinced, in fact, that as useful as she was to me and our children as wife and mother, in that precise moment she was *indispensable* for the little creature being formed in her.

Gianna Beretta Molla, therefore, rested on this evidence of faith: she offered her life aware that without her God could provide for the other children, but that *not even* God could provide for the creature she had in her womb if she rejected it. She was a Christian mother and knew she had to incarnate Providence within her very womb. The rest is entirely entrusted to the name that was given to the fruit of so much sacrifice. While her mother was still on her deathbed, the girl was taken to church and baptized with the name of Gianna Emanuela: the name of her mother together with the name of that Jesus who is God With Us.

Her father then consecrated the girl to Our Lady, as Gianna always loved to do. The family tomb was not ready, and the priest was so moved that he offered the chapel in the middle of the cemetery. So the casket was placed in the tomb of the priests, perhaps a sign of consideration on the part of God, in the face of the sacrifice by this mother.

Servant of God Jérôme Lejeune
GENETIC SCIENTIST
(1926–1994)

A science enthusiast from his childhood, he dedicated himself to the study of Down syndrome, demolishing ancient prejudices. Assisted in part by his Christian sensibility (as an initial form of harmonization between reason and faith), he intuited that speaking of "mongoloid idiocy", as was customary at the time, was a wrong and unjust diagnosis. Attending to those suffering children, he understood that their mental and intellectual processes were affected, but not their humanity, which in certain ways was even more delicate (in memory, in emotion, in sensibility, in sociability, in absence of aggression, and above all in the supremely human capacity of *wonder*).

While studying the formation of the embryo and looking for genetic anomalies, he in fact discovered that at the origin of the disorder was a chromosomal anomaly, which he called "trisomy 21". Later on, in explaining this anomaly, he would use a musical metaphor: "In the symphony that is this human being, there happens what would happen if, in an orchestra, just one musician were to speed up the performance of the piece on his own, disturbing the harmony of the whole." For Lejeune, even the selection of an artistic metaphor in the interest of an explanation was a way of uniting science and charity.

The discovery at first brought him worldwide fame; he received many prestigious international awards, and the professorship in fundamental genetics was created for him at the faculty of medicine in Paris. Convinced he had taken the first basic step toward a possible cure for those children, right in their mother's womb, he afterward discovered to his great sadness that in many countries legislation was being proposed to authorize abortion in the case of the diagnosis of a malformed fetus. This was a distortion of his discovery, and Lejeune fought with all his strength against what he maintained was the "negation of medicine and of all biological fraternity". For this he was marginalized and derided.

An authoritative judgment on his life and testimony has been left for us by another saint who was a contemporary of his, Saint John Paul II, who on the day after his death commemorated him as follows: "Professor Lejeune was always able to employ his profound knowledge of life and of its secrets for the true good of man and of humanity, and only for that purpose. He became one of the most ardent defenders of life, especially of the life of preborn children, which, in our contemporary civilization, is often endangered to such an extent that one could think the danger to be by design. . . . [He] assumed the full responsibility that was his as a scientist. . . . We are faced today with the death of a great Christian of the twentieth century, of a man for whom the defense of life became an apostolate."[13]

In that year of 1994, it was Pope John Paul II himself who had wanted to appoint him as the first president of the Pontifical Academy for Life, in spite of knowing that "his brother Jérôme" was already dying. And he said smiling, with the sense of humor that was habitual for him, "The pope has made an act of hope by appointing a dying man: I will die in 'obligatory service'!"

[13] Letter to Cardinal Lustiger of Paris on April 4, 1994, the day after Professor Lejeune died. www.amislejeune.org/index.php/en/the-cause-of-beatification/testimonies/message-from-pope-john-paul-ii.

On Good Friday of that same year, to the priest who had come to administer the last sacraments to him, he said, "I have never betrayed my faith."

If on his deathbed he had been asked to summarize the Gospel in a single sentence, Lejeune would have answered: "As you did it to one of the least of these my brethren", as Jesus says, "you did it to me" (Mt 25:40).

Servant of God Jacques Fesch
CONDEMNED TO DEATH
(1930–1957)

He was born in France to a prosperous family of Belgian origin. Unfortunately he grew up, as he would later recount, "in a detestable family atmosphere, made of shouting in crucial moments and of discomfort and harshness after crises. No respect, no love! My father, a man who could be charming with outsiders, in fact had a sarcastic, proud, and cynical spirit. An atheist to the extreme, in spite of his professional success, he felt disgust for a life that had brought him nothing but disillusionment and disappointment. From a young age I digested his maxims, nor could I have done otherwise."

He married civilly and had a daughter but abandoned the family in order to give himself over to an empty and disordered life. Having decided to seek adventure in distant Polynesia, he asked his father for the money he needed to buy a boat. At his refusal, he organized a robbery, which ended tragically with the murder of the policeman who was about to arrest him.

While awaiting trial, he was put into solitary confinement in the Santé prison in Paris. He rejected the chaplain who

tried to approach him, but the grace of God reached him
all the same:

> It was one evening, in my cell. . . . In spite of all the catas-
> trophes that had dropped onto my head over the past few
> months, I remained a convinced atheist. . . . Now, that
> evening, I was lying in bed with my eyes open and really
> suffering for the first time in my life with a rare intensity
> over what had been revealed to me concerning certain fam-
> ily matters, and it was then that a cry burst forth from my
> chest, an appeal for help: "My God! My God!" And in-
> stantaneously, like a violent wind that passes without one
> knowing from whence it came, the Spirit of the Lord took
> me by the throat.

His conversion (accompanied by "a powerful and perceptible joy") began with the desire to lead his family members
back to God. So numerous letters began to go out from the
prison, addressed to his father, mother, wife, daughter, in
which he communicated above all the miracle that was happening for him every day: "Now I truly have the certainty
that I am beginning to live for the first time. I have peace
and I have given meaning to my life, while before I was
nothing but one of the living dead."

He turned his prison into a monk's cell and followed a
rule of life with an intense experience of prayer. He read
the life of Saint Thérèse and found it "luminous".

At his trial, he hoped to get some benefit from the testimony of his parents on the sad conditions of his childhood, but his mother died shortly beforehand, and his father showed up drunk.

So Jacques was condemned to death, to the guillotine,
on none other than his birthday. After the initial turmoil of
fear, he discovered deep in his heart the voice of God, who
had been saying to him for some time: "You are receiving

the graces of your death." And he came to this conclusion: "God has taken charge of my little soul." He lived the
months of the tragic countdown meditating on the teaching
of the saint of Lisieux: "All is grace. It is not toward death
that I am going, but toward life."

To his wife and daughter he left a diary-testament, in
which (dated September 10, 1957) he wrote:

> My heart is overflowing with love, especially when I think
> of the holy Virgin. With her I fear nothing, even if I
> should have to suffer a thousand deaths. She protects me
> ceaselessly, and I do not let a quarter of an hour go by
> without addressing prayers and words of love to her. I pic-
> ture her Immaculate Heart all crowned with thorns as she
> showed it to the little shepherds of Fatima, and I dream
> of taking all of those ugly thorns away and healing the
> wounds with kisses. I often repeat to myself the words
> Our Lady spoke to Lucia: "You, at least, try to console
> me!" I often dream of consoling her myself as well.

During his last days, he received as a gift a lock of hair
from his daughter, who was just six years old. He wrote to
her: "What beautiful hair you have! I really have the impression of having my little daughter in the cell!" And to
reassure his daughter and wife, he wrote to them, in the diary, these last words: "Nothing bad will happen to me, and
I will be taken straight to heaven with all the sweetness that
is fitting for a newborn." His wife, Pierrette, to whom he
was married by the Church toward the very end, announced
to him that she would join him by receiving Holy Communion for the first time.

So Jacques was able to write in his diary: "I leave with the
hope that Jesus will soon be in her and that she will finally
believe. I am so happy! May my blood be accepted by God
as a complete sacrifice." He prepared for his execution as
for a martyrdom.

On September 30, 1957, the sixtieth anniversary of the death of Saint Thérèse of the Child Jesus, in his diary he marked down: "Last day of struggle. Tomorrow at this time I will be in heaven. . . . As entirely miserable as I am, I am being given the great honor of being able to imitate our Lord Jesus Christ."

Already in the early hours of that last month, tragic and glorious, he had explained how he would go to meet death: "I hold out one hand to the Virgin and the other to little Thérèse; in this way I run no risk, and they will draw me to themselves."

This beautiful concluding image of a poor man condemned to death who dies as a saint, allowing himself to be led by the hand by the holy Virgin and by little Saint Thérèse of Lisieux, reminds us that what Péguy taught us about the solidarity between saints and sinners also applies (and perhaps most of all) to the dramatic experience of death: "The sinner holds out his hand to the saint, gives his hand to the saint, because the saint gives his hand to the sinner. And all together, the one with the other, the one pulling the other, stretch all the way to Jesus, they make a chain that reaches all the way to Jesus. The one who is not a Christian is the one who does not offer his hand."[14] And Bernanos also reminded us that "we do not die for ourselves, but for each other, or even each in place of another, who knows!"[15]

"None of us lives to himself, and none of us dies to himself. If we live, we live to the Lord, and if we die, we die to

[14] *Un nouveau théologien*, entry dated September 24, 1911, B III (Paris: Gallimard, 1948), p. 573.

[15] Georges Bernanos, *Dialogues des Carmélites*, trans. by Michael Legat, in *The Heroic Face of Innocence: Three Stories* (Grand Rapids, Mich.: Eerdmans, 1999), pp. 73-74.

the Lord; so then, whether we live or whether we die, we are the Lord's. For to this end, Christ died and lived again, that he might be Lord both of the dead and of the living" (Rom 14:7–9).

Marian Conclusion

It would not be right to conclude this book without remembering her who of all saints is Mother and Queen.

The most affectionate way to venerate her seems to me to be that of citing the verses full of tenderness that Dante dedicates to her, describing Our Lady as she rises up to heaven, while the saints reach out for her like children enamored of their mother:

> Here is the rose,
> Wherein the word divine was made incarnate;
> And here the lilies, by whose odour known
> The way of life was follow'd.

~

> Such close was to the circling melody:
> And, as it ended, all the other lights
> Took up the strain, and echoed Mary's name.

~

> And like to babe, that stretches forth its arms
> For very eagerness towards the breast,
> After the milk is taken; so outstretch'd
> Their wavy summits all the fervent band,
> Through zealous love to Mary: then in view
> There halted, and "Regina Coeli" sang
> So sweetly, the delight hath left me never.[1]

---

[1] Dante Alighieri, *Paradise*, trans. H. F. Cary (New York: Hurst, 18--), Canto XXIII.

Index of Saints